Searching for a Stranger and

Finding Myself

A Memoir

Wendy L. Scott-Hawkins

Dedicated to those still searching

Laurie
I hope you enjoy my
book and can take one
thing away from it to
enhance your life.

Wendy Scott

CONTENTS

AUTHOR'S NOTE

I'm writing this memoir to document the factual, intriguing account of my humble life and the search for my forgotten half-brother. When I explain my quest, people usually say, "That sounds like a movie!" or "Your life has been so exciting!" Although I highly doubt it's filled with enough action, adventure, and thrills to be a movie script, this book certainly contains many unbelievable coincidences and startling events.

This story offers a chronological account of the many happy, heart-breaking, and inspirational moments that occurred during my search. Although I'm no expert on searching for adoptees, I can say countless hours were spent looking for someone I didn't even know but felt drawn to find.

For those of you searching for an adopted family member or loved one, read on for inspiration and for information to help with planning your search. And for those of you just here for a good story, you're in for quite the adventure ... please buckle up, ease back in your seats, and enjoy the ride of my life.

PREFACE

July 21, 1967

They call me their little girl and I love it. I know I'm spoiled by these three old ladies from the parsonage, and my sisters are jealous. They tell me so. No matter. They have people spoiling them too. We each get to live at different houses while Mom goes to big school for a while.

It's Friday night and that means one of two things: heading to the States for supper and shopping or staying home and playing games. They have decided it's shopping. Yes. I'm happy about their decision. Crossing that big bridge from Canada to the States is scary, so I duck down in the backseat until we are completely over. Jean slips me an American dollar to spend. "That's a lot of money," she says, "so remember to save some." I can't help myself. I blow it all. I feel a little guilty, but after all it was my money to spend. Another colouring book and crayons were just what I needed.

We cross the big, long bridge and are home again. I feel sleepy. My snack tonight is cheese and crackers with only a few black licorice candies. Why can't I have more candies?

I brush my teeth and climb into bed. The sheets smell so fresh and clean. Miss Barber must have done laundry today and hung my sheets out. I watch the curtains gently blow in the summer breeze. Jean sleeps in the bed next to me and likes to have the window open, even in the winter. That's not allowed at my other house. "We're not heating the outside," they'd tell me.

We all say our prayers together and sing a song about birds up in a treetop. I don't remember finishing the song, which Jean confirms the next morning. She teases me about how I didn't sing my part. When my turn came up I was sawing logs.

They don't have any children of their own, so I plan on teaching them everything. Last night, I even showed Jean how to put my diaper on. She would be lost without me.

When I'm at their house I play with friends I've made down the street. One little girl has real Barbies (I know they are real because the legs bend) and all kinds of clothes and shoes to dress them up in. Her Barbie even has a house of her own and a car to drive. Mom says Santa isn't real, so her parents must buy her all this stuff. They must be really rich. And I know she is spoiled by the way she bosses me around. Still, it's nice to have real toys to play with, and not have to pretend, so I stay quiet and don't stand up to her.

July 22, 1967

It's Saturday so Jean isn't working at the hardware store and Dorothy won't be going to Androck. Sometimes I go with Jean to the store and learn all about hardware stuff like nuts and bolts and how to cut glass. She doesn't work tomorrow either as Sunday is the Lord's day and we'll be going to church and mostly resting.

Miss Barber is home every day but will be working on her talk for church tomorrow. She is the minister at the church beside their house. Her study, the one with the accordion door, is full of all sorts of junk she calls important papers. I don't know how she even moves around in there let alone finds anything. She plays the piano and the accordion. I like it when she plays the accordion and maybe someday she'll let me give it a try. I practice the piano and my preaching when I go to the church to play. It's fun doing whatever I want to do there.

One day last week when Jean stopped in at the hardware store, I waited in the car. It was parked in front of the store so she could still see me. I think she calls the car a Volkswagen. I was turning the wheel back and forth fast, pretending I was driving. She didn't say I couldn't touch anything so I was pressing shiny things, pulling handles, and using the blinker thing. I was even making loud noises like the car was going fast. Vrooom, vroom.

The next thing I knew, I was going backward and Jean was running alongside me trying to open the door. She finally got it open and stopped the car but boy was I ever scared. I wasn't in trouble, though, and we laughed about it at supper that night.

Since it's Saturday, there is plenty of work to do. Dorothy is home on the weekends so she usually joins Jean and me outside. Miss Barber does stuff in the house like baking pies. I've watched her before, but she doesn't ask for my help. She likes her soap operas playing on the TV while she's ironing. I like to see the steam from the iron and hear the hiss as she presses the clothes.

In the past, I have helped out with many of the outdoor chores like gardening (my least favourite), cracking walnuts with a hammer, picking apples, scraping old furniture with a piece of glass, and picking up sticks around the yard. As for indoor chores, I mainly watch, as they usually involve the hot gas stove and making stuff to put in jars for canning or bags for freezing. My favourite time in the kitchen is at Christmas. I like to sample the Nuts and Bolts, fudge, and Christmas pudding.

Today we decide to work in the garden and then possibly go fishing after lunch. At lunch, Jeans says, "Eat, Pete." I think it's funny when she calls me Pete, but it does make me eat instead of talk. Today's lunch is my favourite: ooey, gooey grilled cheese sandwiches. The cheese seems endless when I take a bite, so I twirl it around my finger to break it.

I wait patiently after I finish my sandwich, but I keep staring up at the wooden boat hanging on the wall thinking about our fishing adventure. The boat has little shelves perfect for holding a single piece of Double Bubble gum. Jean always has one sitting on the little shelf and there is one there today. Yes. She finally notices and offers it to me. I smile and thank her.

Off we go to the pond for some fishing. It's the one where Jean tells me I can only catch one or two. At the other pond, I can catch as many as I want. Before long, I have one on. Jean yells, "Red, get the net!", and Dorothy comes running with the net to scoop up my fish. Afterward, the man weighs it and Jean gives him money. I wish I could stay here all day. The fish are easy to catch and I don't have to wait long for a bite. Jean cleans the fish when we get home and cooks it for supper. She says it's a trout. Either way, it's very tasty. I like to fish and to catch them all by myself.

Tonight's game is my choice so I pick Crokinole. That's the one where you hold your fingers a certain way and flick the middle one so it hits the round playing piece. It hurts your finger sometimes, but the game is so much fun. If you flick your finger at just the right speed, your piece slides ever so smoothly and gently until it lands in the centre hole. That's worth a lot of points. We have church tomorrow, so it's off to bed early.

July 23, 1967

Today is a special day ... it's my fourth birthday! I hope the three ladies remember and surprise me with a gift. I hope I get a real Barbie doll.

It's Sunday morning and Dorothy is dressed in her best dress for church. She also wears a pair of tall boots. She tells me if she doesn't wear the boots, Bimbo will scratch her nylons and make runs in them. That darn cat is so mean. She likes to scratch me as well, but maybe I shouldn't tease her with my housecoat belt. When I wiggle it on the floor, Bimbo pounces on it. Sometimes she gets my hands with her claws if I don't pull the belt away fast enough. I guess they keep her because she's so pretty, gray, and fluffy.

My dress, a hand-me-down, is from one of Jean's nieces. The three girls are older than me so I get their old clothes when they are done with them. I don't mind because the clothes are nice and new to me. Sometimes it seems like Christmas when I open the boxes filled with their old clothes. I get excited to try them on. Yellow and blue are my favourite colours so those are my first pick. I'm told because of my red hair, I shouldn't wear pink, red, or purple. I'll give the clothes of those colours to my sisters, Wanda and Linda, along with any others that don't fit. Some of the clothes I keep here and some I take home. Dresses aren't my favourite thing to wear, but since it's Sunday I know I have to wear one.

Sitting through church on a hard pew feels like an eternity. I'd rather be outside fishing, riding my bike, or hanging out with Jean. She secretly slips me a candy called a Humbug. I love candy as much as I love bubble gum. It's a wonder I have any teeth left.

Miss Barber preaches on and on and I feel restless. I try to keep still but my butt hurts from sitting so long and I start to wiggle around. "Just a little longer," I tell myself. Jean just looks ahead or smiles down at me once in a while. If Mom were here, she would have pinched my leg by now and given me the "sit still" look.

Finally, we sing a song and it's over. After saying goodbye to everyone we head next door for lunch. Afterwards, Jean lets me help roll the money from the offering. I love counting the shiny change, hearing it jingle in my palm, and feeling its coolness on my fingers when touching it. I feel important, pretending this is my job and I'm a grown-up.

Sunday afternoons I always have a long nap here. I wake to the sweet smell of chocolate cake. I rush downstairs and find Miss Barber adding the finishing touches to a double-layer cake with mounds of chocolate icing. They did remember after all. We have all my favourite foods for supper and then I open my gifts. I carefully unwrap each one and am hopeful that the long one is the Barbie. It's not. It's another fake. I hide my disappointment and sincerely say, "Thank you." I know the importance of being polite.

Another day is done. We say our prayers again and sing about the birds in the treetop. I love staying here with the three old ladies, but I miss my family and wish I was home.

July 25, 1967

Today, the three ladies from the parsonage and I walk into the funeral home in Strathroy, Ontario. Something doesn't feel right. They are very quiet when we enter the awful smelling place. I don't know why we are here. I love and trust these ladies and know they care for me deeply. So why do I feel alone and uneasy? My stomach churns and I feel sick. What is this I'm feeling? Maybe stress and anxiety. One of the ladies signs my name to the register. My fourth birthday was two days ago, so maybe they think I'm too young to sign it on my own.

Looking around, I see strangers but also some of my family members. My mom and sisters are here ... so why am I not with them? My heart feels like it's being torn in two. I want to scream to get their attention. Instead, I push my feelings down and hide them away so no one knows how I feel. I say nothing. I remain calm. This way, I can't get hurt, right? If nobody knows then everything is fine. Life goes on as usual. And anyway, who is the person in that bed at the front of the room? Should I know him? Maybe that's why we are here.

I really know things aren't right when later I go back to the parsonage with Miss Barber, Dorothy, and Jean ... NOT with my family.

PART ONE

BEFORE THE SEARCH

CHAPTER ONE

SHOT IN THE HEART

July 22, 1967

A young woman was heard screaming and seen running down the street during the early morning hours of this fateful summer day. She would later have to be sedated after police questioned her for several hours about the shooting death of her boyfriend Leonard Hawkins. Leonard had been killed at the home where she had been staying in London, Ontario.

Nancy, a pretty blonde in her mid-teens, had somehow become involved with Leonard, a married man. Her father had died when she was young, leaving her mother with several children to raise. This may have been why Nancy was looking for love in all the wrong places.

She met Leonard and instantly fell in love. Even knowing he was already married to Jean Hawkins (born

Meadows) and had three very young girls didn't stop her from pursuing him. Against all odds, he left his wife and children to be with her. Little did she know, at this young age, habits die hard. Leonard had been unfaithful to his wife, was young and attractive, and wasn't about to change his ways. He liked to go on all-night benders with his buddies and enjoyed a single man's lifestyle. He didn't want to answer to anybody but himself.

Their relationship together was short-lived, lasting only for a few years. In that time, they travelled west for a number of possible reasons, such as being near to his extended family, finding work, or hiding something like a pregnancy. Yes, Nancy had become pregnant while under the age of 18, so now was going to have a child to take care of.

Things hadn't gone as planned for Nancy. Her current bed was the living room couch of Leonard's friends, the Robys. Her relationship with Leonard had become rocky and they were separated. She stayed with this young couple, and their three children, while she decided her next move.

On July 22, 1967, the story of Leonard's death made the front page of a London newspaper and included a sketch depicting the crime scene. The diagram added more interest to the story as it traced the movements of Leonard and Nancy during the last minutes of his life.

The article claimed that Leonard had been out to a hotel with friends the night of July 21 and had cruised by the Roby residence earlier that evening. Later, at some point, he left the hotel and went to the Robys' house where he broke in and found Nancy on the couch asleep. He shook her awake and threatened to kill her. Nancy fled, running into the Robys' bedroom for help. Mr. Roby grabbed his gun, searched his house, and then called the police. While Mr. Roby was dialing the last digit, Leonard ran back into the house and charged at him. Leonard grabbed the barrel of the gun and punched Mr. Roby. During the struggle, the gun went off and a bullet slammed into Leonard's chest. In shock, Leonard ran to the bed, where he fell and died right in front of Mrs. Roby and Nancy. Fortunately, the three children in the home were spared the memory as they were asleep at the time.

Mr. Roby was later taken to the police station, questioned, and then released. No charges were laid but the newspaper stated there would be an inquest. The article ended with a brief mention of Leonard being separated from his wife and three daughters.

This was something neither Nancy nor the Robys would ever forget. All three were witnesses to his death. Shock, disbelief, and later regret would surely all play a part in their lives. No doubt the game "What if" played across their minds for years. Based on the witness testimony given by Nancy and the Robys, the shooting was classified as self-defense. But really, they could tell the story any way they liked. Who would ever know but them?

Leonard's family members speculated if the truth had been told. Myrna, Leonard's youngest sister, attended the inquest where the jury found the shooting completely accidental. This verdict was reached after coroner and police reports were presented along with the witness testimonies. She remembers there being no mention of a baby at the Roby house that night. It was understood that Nancy had given up the baby some weeks before the shooting.

It sounds fairly reasonable for the jury to reach a decision based on the evidence and testimonies. If someone grabs the barrel of a loaded firearm, I guess we shouldn't be surprised if the gun accidentally goes off. For Leonard, though, it was the last mistake he'd ever make in a string of bad decisions.

What was Leonard thinking that night? Possibly he wanted to see Nancy to try to make things right with her. Maybe she had decided it wasn't going to work out for them, and when he shook her awake from a deep sleep she didn't want any part of a reconciliation. His history of drinking had turned him into a violent and abusive man, and I'm sure he demanded to see his child. There is no mention of a baby in the newspaper article, but possibly it was omitted or withheld due to extenuating circumstances. Nancy being underage when she conceived the baby could have caused other problems. So when Leonard woke Nancy and they argued, he likely threatened to kill her. And she knew Leonard well enough to run and get Mr. Roby. Nancy knew when Leonard was drunk there was no reasoning with him.

The newspaper article alluded to the fact that Leonard had broken into the home. Again, what was he thinking? You can't just break into a house, threaten to kill someone, and think everything will turn out fine. If he had been out drinking all night and was driving while intoxicated, added on to all the other offences he had just committed, he would be facing some serious charges.

Of course, Leonard wouldn't have the opportunity to have his day in court. His life ended on July 22, 1967, at 4:15 a.m. He really did die hard. He was only twenty-five years old and left behind four children, all under five years of age. It was a tragic incident that changed many lives for years to come.

So what does all this have to do with me?

CHAPTER TWO

LEFT BEHIND

Present Day

Leonard Wesley Hawkins was my father. I was one of the four children he left behind so suddenly and tragically.

His funeral was the confusing event I attended on July 25, 1967, with the three ladies. I happened to be staying at the parsonage when he was killed—on the day before my fourth birthday. I don't remember much else, but I do remember it didn't feel right to be at the funeral home without my mom and sisters. They were my real family and I loved and missed them. My dad had left our family when I was around two years old, so I didn't understand the significance of who was lying in the coffin. In my mind he was already gone, so it's no wonder I was confused. I'm sure the ladies told me who he was, but the meaning of "father" without a father figure in my life would have been foreign to me. To this day, the word has no real meaning for me. Your father, our father, and my father are ways my family and I talk about him. But to me, he is like a person from a fairytale as I have no real vivid memories of him.

Sometimes now, I try to conjure up memories of my dad but the only one I have, and it's more like a dream, is hiding behind a door with a mirror on the back of it. In my mind I think I am at Grandpa and Grandma Hawkins' house in Strathroy and I need to be quiet; kind of like when you are playing hide and seek. A recent conversation with my sister Wanda has narrowed this event down to a time when our drunken father came and picked us up from our grandparent's home. Someone must have tried hiding us there, but he demanded to take his daughters. Afterwards, he dropped us off at one of his friend's houses, took off, and they called my grandparents or mother to come and pick us up. He must have been with Nancy at the time but wanted to see us. I guess he just went about it the wrong way and never really had any intentions of spending time with us that day. Remember, drink and Leonard did not mix.

So who was Leonard before he fell into the bottle? Lenoard (spelled this way on his birth certificate but nowhere else) Wesley Hawkins was born January 13, 1942, in Sudbury, Ontario. His driver's licence states he was five feet eight inches tall, which was an average height for a man back then. His hair was jet black and kept neat and tidy. His appearance meant a lot to him. He has been described by both men and women as very handsome. He liked to do push-ups and other exercises, which may have been how he maintained his trim physique. His job classification for the National Employment Service listed him as a labourer. This is no surprise as he enjoyed working with his hands. He liked to do woodworking, automotive painting, and gardening. When I look at photographs of him, he seems very handsome and reminds me of Elvis Presley. I wouldn't be shocked if he thought this himself.

Avoiding the truth seemed easy for Leonard. When he and my mom first met, he wouldn't tell her his name until they started dating. She didn't want to go out with him at first. She told me he acted tough, was in a gang with other hoods (they used chains as weapons to beat up rival gang members), and had tattoos. One of the tattoos was a "V" for Victory and the other was the initials of a former girlfriend. Leonard's gang life resulted in some trouble with the law at an early age. His parents were shocked by his behaviour as Leonard's siblings were on the straight and narrow path. I've been told he wouldn't look for a fight but never backed down from one either. His reputation for winning subjected him to many sporadic brawls. Everywhere he went, people wanted to fight him.

Up until they got married, my mother thought Leonard was the same age as her or older. It turns out he was only eighteen when they married and she was twenty. He revealed this fact on their wedding day when they were signing the register. It was too late for her to turn back. This was the first of many "stunts," as my mom called them, he would pull during their marriage.

Regardless, my mom loved him and was ready to settle down and have children right away. Being a beautiful brunette with a shapely figure allowed her to date many young men before settling down with my dad. Her father warned her not to marry him because "He was a no-good bum!" but she did so anyways against his will.

Leonard's love for ladies would prove he never should have been married at the young age of eighteen. Mom tells me he would "run around with women." Frustrated and hurt, she left him once just after having Wanda and went back home to her parents. He called, begging her to come back, and of course, she conceded. This would continue throughout their marriage, but somehow he knew enough to be home when she was ready to deliver another baby. There is a picture of him holding me as a newborn and his head is shaved. I still haven't figured that one out. Mom says she told him he looked dumb.

When I look at their wedding pictures, they appear to be happy and well-matched. Who could guess this lovely couple would face so many challenges during the short time they were married? Within four years they had three children. Mom explained to me that back then, "You got married and had kids. There was no planning and thinking about their education. You just had kids because that's what you did."

Mom said Dad would give us horsey rides on his back and play with us. "He was good to you girls; holding and taking care of you. He loved you all very much!" and "He really tried." She recalls him saying to us girls, "You do what your mother says," so I feel he respected Mom's values and opinions on raising us by stating it openly to us.

Dad's younger sister, Aunt Myrna, was a teenager at the time of his marriage. She had yet to be married or have any children. She looked up to her older brother and loved coming over to help out with us three girls. She had black hair like her brother, and similar but very feminine, attractive facial features. Her fair complexion contrasted starkly with her dark hair, but it made her a real beauty. She once told me, in her soft-spoken manner, how she had enjoyed watching Dad teach us how to brush our teeth before bed. Having nice white clean teeth was an essential part of his routine. She also shared, "People loved him. He was polite, handsome, and intelligent but had a wild side to him. He never had the chance to outgrow that." Leonard was the perfect big brother in her eyes.

Being quiet, reserved, withdrawn, and uncommunicative are personality traits that explain why my father never spoke of his feelings. But I have to wonder if men even did that back then, tell how they felt. If he did confide in someone that person was not my mother. She said, "He never talked to me. Never told me what he was thinking." She does recall one time, though, he blurted out, "I hate my dad!" Maybe if he had dealt with some of his demons, things would have been different.

I picture my dad as being very easy-going and having a carefree spirit. It would probably take a lot to rattle his chain and maybe Mom would do just that when he wasn't contributing to the household by holding down a job. Or maybe she would become so exasperated when he returned from his drinking binges with friends that she just blew up at him. Mom was working and caring for three young children. This must have been exhausting. Between the unemployment, drinking, money problems, infidelity, and inexperience at solving marital issues, is it any wonder they couldn't save their marriage?

My sister Wanda, being the oldest, remembers the fights between our parents and the empty cupboards. Linda and I have been spared these memories due to our young ages. My mom told me she sometimes brought us girls to her in-laws for dinner just so we could get a decent meal. "There was no food in the cupboard," she told me matter of factly, "What else was I to do?"

Dad handled the situation by escaping it, stepping out of his marriage, meeting Nancy, getting her pregnant, and later dying a senseless death on a bed in the Roby home. Mom, on the other hand, had surrendered her life to Jesus Christ near the end of their marriage and Leonard had noticed the change. He told her she was different and I'm sure she was. Maybe he didn't like the person she had become, or maybe he knew he couldn't fill the role of a Christian's husband?

To save her dignity, my mother considered herself widowed, even though they had been separated for a few years by this point. I believe she had hopes that even after everything he had done, she would have the opportunity to forgive him and take him back. She saw him walking down the street a week before his death and he completely ignored her. That was the last time she saw him alive. She had heard that he went to jail for unpaid fines in the time they were apart, and she wished he hadn't been bailed out. I remember her saying, "Maybe he would still be alive today if he had remained in jail."

Newspaper articles and radio coverage about my father's shooting were released before my mother was officially informed about his death. Aunt Jane, Grandpa Meadows' sister, heard it on the news and told Mom about his passing. She had been staying with Aunt Jane while she was in London completing her upgrading. It seems odd that many people knew about it before my mom and his daughters—his closest family. This wasn't an appropriate way for Mom to find out about his death. The police should have notified her first before it was released to the media even if Mom and Dad were separated.

My mother had difficulty coping with his death. Her doctor prescribed medication quite freely and with no real long-term goal. She never attended grief counselling or joined a support group. I'm not sure if they even had those kinds of resources available back then. We sure have come a long way since then in terms of mental health support. My mother eventually had what was referred to as a "nervous breakdown" and did spend some time with a psychiatrist. Nowadays she would have been diagnosed with a mental health condition such as depression or anxiety. Decades ago, sadly there were way fewer answers and a lot less support.

For my mother, it was an ongoing battle to stay afloat each day, and nighttime was even more difficult. More and more pills became her answer, until suddenly these concoctions were a part of her daily life.

Given that mental illness can be hereditary and is exacerbated by environmental factors, I guess it's unsurprising to most that I've also experienced the disease firsthand. Being raised by someone struggling with mental illness was a challenge to say the least … but more on that and how I survived it later.

CHAPTER THREE

BACK AND FORTH

July 1967

The parsonage stood alongside the Pentecostal church in Arkona, Ontario. This would be my home during the week, and then I'd reunite with my mom and two sisters at our grandparent's home on the weekend. My two sisters Wanda and Linda also spent their weeks at different homes and then rejoined the family on the weekend. Wanda was five years old, Linda was two, and I was turning four on July 23.

During my stay at the parsonage, I lived with three middle-aged spinsters, two of whom were pastors of the adjacent church. I felt very loved, wanted, and spoiled by their affection and attention. Miss Barber, Dorothy, and Jean had no children of their own and had never married.

This arrangement had come to fruition after my mom

separated from my father and returned to Adult Learning in London. Jean Hawkins had married young and with only a grade nine education realized she needed more schooling to better support her three girls. Before marrying, she worked as a waitress, factory labourer, dietary aide, and personal attendant in a nursing home. During her marriage and three pregnancies, she was a cashier at the A & P grocery store in Strathroy. This was short for The Great Atlantic and Pacific Tea Company.

As I mentioned, our home on the weekends was with Mom's parents, Grandpa and Grandma Meadows, at their house on Arkona's main street. Many hours were spent on the front porch, counting or watching the cars go by. They had taken us in since the separation and it made transitioning from house to house easier with little travel involved for us girls. Wanda and Linda's guardians were Grandma Meadows' sisters Fay and Alice. They each had spouses and were empty nesters, so they could offer my sisters the love and attention they deserved.

Linda's weekday home was situated on a farm, several miles west of Arkona. She spent lots of time outdoors, playing with the barn kittens and eating strawberries from the well-established berry patch.

Wanda's guardians lived on the outskirts of Arkona and owned the town's gas station and coffee shop. She spent her days helping out there, learning valuable cooking and customer service skills.

We split up our time like this for approximately two

years until Mom graduated. We were all very young little ladies whose lives so far had been filled with anything but normalcy.

My life during those two years with my grandparents was far from wonderful. Grandpa Meadows (Frederick or Ted for short) liked his drink but was a hard worker. He had his own poultry business where he moved chickens from barns to businesses—we called it the "chicken catching" business. To say that I disliked him would be an understatement. We were taught not to hate anyone so I guess that choice was out. He did not keep his anger in check. Instead, he transferred it to others. Mom said it was just the way he was. But looking back now, I think he was just plain mean.

I was tasked with helping Grandpa Meadows keep up appearances. I remember having to massage Grecian Formula through his dirty hair. It always seemed greasy and stinky. Maybe that was part of the dying process, but it sure wasn't pleasant. I also had to apply black shoe polish to his shoes or boots and then buff them with a stiff brush.

Sometimes his meanness became physical. One time when my elbow was on the dinner table he hit it hard with his fork. "Get your elbows off the table. This is not a horses stable," will be forever embedded in my mind as he directed his anger at me. His actions and words not only hurt me physically but mentally as well. At the time

I was a petite child, but that didn't matter to him. I was still fair game.

Since Grandpa had lived through the depression, any kind of food waste was wrong in his books. I hated the texture of fat on meat and thought it was disgusting. He would demand everyone at the table to finish all the food on their plate and bullied me into eating a grizzly, greasy, lump of lard. I felt he was being intentionally nasty to me, and yelled, "You are going to Hell!" I don't remember any more disputes between us after that. In 1972, when I was nine years old, he died of a heart attack at age sixty-one. Maybe it was from eating all that fat.

Grandma Meadows (Evelyn) experienced a lot of abuse at the hands of her husband, but she stayed with him until the end. That's what you did back then, as divorce was rarely an option. You stuck it out for better or for worse. Even as a young child I remember wondering, "How does she put up with him? He is so mean." Grandma always appeared calm and would say, "Now Ted," followed by whatever he needed help with to settle down.

She was everybody's Grandma and the neighbourhood children even called her that. I was a little jealous of this at the time but not enough to stop me from playing with them. With her round face, plump figure, and desire to give away cookies, she resembled Mrs. Claus except for her dark hair. Everyone was welcome in her home and she always made you feel comfortable around her long log kitchen table. Her kindness and generosity stemmed from her steadfast faith in God and attending church.

Her sons (five in total) always respected her and showed her affection through their playful antics. Uncle Ron used to hide her purse in the freezer and then ask, "Hey Ev, you want some cold cash?" She loved this attention and would ask, "Now Ron. What have you done with my purse?" smiling the whole time. In my high school graduation year of 1981, when I was seventeen, she died of a heart attack. Grandma was seventy years old when she died. And had nine years of life on her own after Grandpa died. I wonder if she ate the fat on her meat during those nine years, or if she threw it in the garbage where it belonged.

Arkona was a very small village at the time, with a population of under 500, so everybody knew everybody. Rock Glen Falls was the main attraction and many tourists and archeologists travelled to see its beauty, Carolinian forest, and fossils. It was located a few miles north of Arkona on a hilly dirt road. You know, the kind where you leave your stomach behind if travelling at a high velocity and can feel yourself lifting off the seat. Lots of fun on a school bus. Other than Rock Glen, Arkona had nothing to offer in the way of entertainment. So we just made our own with what very little resources we had. I remember a lot of pretending this and pretending that. Kids nowadays would certainly not last a day in the Arkona of my childhood.

My red hair and freckled face distinguished me from my sisters who were both blonde. It's been a long-standing joke that I was a product of the milkman or possibly one of Mom's doctors as neither of my parents had red hair. Research shows red hair does skip a generation or two sometimes and that's what I'm going with. My Mom's grandpa, Harry Cochrane, had red hair so this is enough for me to believe the research theory and all that recessive gene stuff.

Of course, with red hair being so uncommon, I stood out like a sore thumb. I was teased by other children and given my lack of self-confidence I was not emotionally equipped to handle these situations. Some of the names I recall being flung at me are Rusty, Red, and Ginger. I wanted to crawl under a table or run away and hide every time I was called one of these names. I did not like being defined by the colour of my hair or my freckles.

Adults joined in on the barrage of names even though they must have known I didn't like it, especially when they commented on my flushed face. They didn't have to point this out as I could feel the heat emanating from my skin. I remember turning fifty shades of red (no, not grey) whenever I was centred out or asked questions by an adult such as a teacher. Long sleeves in the heat of summer only caused more unwanted attention, but I thought it would cover up my bright freckles that only multiplied with sun exposure. My theory was, "Out of sight, out of mind."

On top of the red hair and freckles, I was shy and extremely self-conscious. My friends and family were the exception. I was quite talkative and comfortable while in conversations with them, but I still didn't want to show vulnerability by crying over little things like emotions. You had to physically hurt me before I'd show any signs of pain. My decimated self-worth and unstable family life didn't allow me to expect the love and understanding I deserved. I became really good at shrugging off emotional and physical pain.

My personality was shaped by the people and events leading up to this point in my life. If I had to continue the way I was going, how would I ever survive?

CHAPTER FOUR

NEAR DISASTERS

1967-1977

When Mom told us we had a half-sibling, I was shocked. She wasn't, though, given my father's philandering. "Only one that I know of, but who knows ... there could be more." She was never told by my father's family whether it was a girl or a boy and she didn't ask. It would have been too hurtful. After all, he had left her to be with Nancy, and we all know hell hath no fury like a woman scorned. Furious, seething with rage and jealousy, livid, breathing fire, and resentful are fairly good representations of how I would have felt in my mom's situation.

We had two adopted cousins on mom's side of the family. Our relatives couldn't have children of their own so they adopted a boy and a girl. Whenever our adopted sibling came up in conversation, my mother would say she thought the girl could be her. She resembled my younger sister Linda, with her dirty blonde hair, round face, fair complexion and she was about the same age our mystery sibling would be. I always wondered if it was her.

Thoughts of what happened to the baby and Nancy would occasionally cross my mind, even more so as time passed. After the shooting, Nancy didn't have my dad around to help raise the baby, and being so young, I wondered how she could have possibly raised the child by herself. She must not have had a great support system seeing as she had been living with my dad's friends until she could get on her feet. She would have had no choice but to put the baby up for adoption and hope it went to a good family, or muddle through and try to find another man to help her out.

My mysterious half-sibling was never discussed when we visited our dad's family during summer vacation and Christmas holidays. I guess, though, what would they say? "Hey girls. Do you ever wonder about that illegitimate half-sibling of yours?" No, it was definitely a hush-hush kind of thing. A family disaster not to be spoken of ever again, until …

At this point, before I get into the details of my search for my half-sibling, I need to share more of my personal history. This background information will show my determined nature was not something I grew into as an adult. Rather, it was a part of me from a very young age. Tough and even at times disastrous situations forced me to learn to sink or swim, but also opened up opportunities for growth. We often hear about people who carry the burdens of their childhood with them throughout their life and dwell on the negative. Not me. There is no doubt I suffered, but overcoming those hurdles has made me into the positive woman I am today.

Life without a father seemed perfectly normal to me at the time. I didn't know any different. My dad had been gone for so long, I had no idea what I was missing. Sure, it was darn awkward when Father's Day came around and kids at school made their dads cards. But honestly, it was no big deal. I just accepted it.

We rented a small, one-and-a-half storey home from the three parsonage ladies for most of my childhood, and I felt secure knowing where my head would land each night. The neighbourhood had other families with children my age, so there were some children, other than my two sisters, for me to play with. Arkona did have some single-parent families, but they were few and far between. I can count on one hand how many I remember. Most were the typical two-parent variety.

Grandpa and Grandma Meadows lived on the main street and we usually stopped there on the way "uptown" to get a cookie from Grandma. Mom sought refuge at her parent's house frequently and developed a close bond with her mom. She also loved her father dearly because she respected him. Earlier, I shared my opinion of him, and obviously there was no love lost between us. Back then, at least in my case, most family members lived close by. The Meadows family had six children in total. Some were married and had children of their own around my age. Nearly all of them lived in Arkona or within a half hour drive. As a result we were a tight-knit bunch. I enjoyed hanging out with my cousins, even if sometimes they were a bad influence.

"Hey Wendy, how about we paint my trailer black? I know how to do it. It's so easy. Do you want to help?" My cousin Warren Meadows lived in a trailer park near Sarnia, Ontario, and he had decided that their pink mobile trailer would look better black. So while on a visit there one summer, he got out the necessary equipment, which back then was just paint and a paintbrush, and proceeded to paint the trailer. I remember watching him laying on the ground and painting underneath it. Being only about four at the time, one year younger than myself, he looked so small under the big trailer. Oh my goodness. The black looked so dark over the pink! But I picked up a brush and helped. I'm not sure how far we got, but by the time his dad caught us, the damage was done. He got a lickin' but I was spared. Seeing as he was a troublemaker, he would have been blamed and not his innocent cousin. Ironically, Warren went on to be a pro-fessional painter and now has a very profitable business.

That story could have ended a lot worse if we hadn't gotten caught early in the job. In the next story you will see I was saved from disaster by a much higher power. Winter always brought lots of snow, which seemed to stay forever. I couldn't wait until spring, when I could ditch the heavy, winter boots and wear my running shoes. Thankfully the cold winter days were at least sunny, which made the long months bearable.

On one such sunny winter day, my friend Donna and I went for a Ski-doo ride in a field adjacent to my yard. She was about ten years old and I was thirteen. Her brothers told her to stick to the path they had packed down during their previous rides, but Donna had other plans.

My feet were snug and warm in my brand new (not handed down!) ankle height, black leather boots so at first I was a happy rider. But then I saw tall grass-like things sticking out of the snow and realized she was veering off the snow-packed path. I tried yelling at her over the noise of the engine. She motioned that everything was fine.

The next thing I knew ... whomp ... the sled came to an abrupt stop in deep snow and water. We thought we were sinking. Donna's nose was bleeding and she kept wiping it with her white fur mitts. We both panicked and tried to climb above the snow, but it seemed just too high and soft.

Eventually, we made it to safety and walked home,

feet soaking wet, heads hanging with shame and regret. Donna was grounded from driving the Ski-doo for a while and my new boots were never the same after all that water.

It took quite a few men and muscle to lift the sled out of the hole. Things could have been a whole lot worse, but God's hand had been upon us. Not far from the spot we went in was a much deeper part of the pond. The story would have ended in disaster if we had gone in there.

CHAPTER FIVE

SISTERHOOD THROUGH POVERTY

1967-1977

We didn't have much money, but our little white house stood on a corner lot, so we did have the best yard in the neighbourhood for meeting up and playing in. Most times we started games at our house, such as hide'n' seek, but would branch out to other yards from there. I remember practicing for school track and field in our yard, racing against the bigger boy next door. It helped prepare me physically and mentally for competition against the girls in my division. Although running and skipping were my favourite outdoor activities, I have fond memories of just sitting on the grass looking for four-leaf clovers with our neighbour, Mrs. Ridley, who lived kitty-corner to us. She made it seem so interesting that everyone wanted to get in on the search. It was nearly impossible to find one, but that didn't stop me from trying. And it did kill plenty of hours when there wasn't much else to do.

Mother's and Widow's Allowance brought us up to the poverty level, plus Mom worked at the local grocery store on Saturdays to help supplement her income. It was on those Saturdays that my sister Linda and I discovered pie and neapolitan ice cream made a terrific breakfast. One time, when there was only one huge piece of pie left in the container, Linda found it first and wouldn't share. I told her it was big enough for both of us if she cut it in half, but she wanted it all. She ate the whole thing right out of the container and later regretted it when she felt sick. I reminded her of that sick feeling and the importance of sharing for years.

Linda and I also loved watching Saturday morning cartoons while eating delectable desserts for breakfast. We would watch and eat for as long as our older sister Wanda let us. Cartoons would be on television from early morning until noon. Back then, you couldn't record, PVR, YouTube, or buy shows, so you had to watch them when they were on. Wanda, though, had a different agenda. Being the oldest, she was in charge and played the role of boss very well. She would write a list of chores for us and then check them off when they were completed. We hated it but did as we were told.

One bike for all three of us girls to share, a handful of board games, no name Barbie dolls, and hand me downs all revealed our limited budget. We had to wait for everything until we could afford it. Our lack of toys did, however, result in better imaginations. We had to pretend and make things to compensate for what we didn't have. Examples of this are many. We pretended the swings from our swingset were guitars and used the clotheslines for volleyball. Another time, Linda and I imagined kitchen chairs were horses and tried riding them up the stairs. We didn't get far before we realized this wasn't such a great idea. Tumbling backwards kind of gave this away. Let's just say chrome chairs are not very forgiving.

It was always about reinventing or replacing what we didn't have to make our lives work. This formed a strong family bond. Anyone who knew us sensed how close we were, and still are. Don't get me wrong. The necessities such as food and shelter were always supplied, but any extras were longed for until the right time. Did it hurt me? Absolutely not. Now, I appreciate everything that comes my way and work hard for it.

"Door number one, two, or three?" was challenged by one of us girls to the others. As the only parent, Mom would tire of us by evening and be more than ready to put us to bed. It would still be daylight and we were wide awake so we used to make up games to play. The door game was one we could play while lying in bed. The person designated "It" would think of three males ranging from really homely to absolutely gorgeous and put one behind each door. The "Guesser" would then pick a door to reveal their boyfriend. Fits of laughter would erupt if you chose the door that represented the homely man, and before long Mom would yell, "Quiet down up there! You girls get to sleep." We would quiet down, but only until the next round of gameplay. Then there would be more yelling, as well as threats like, "Be quiet or I'm coming up with the belt," which Mom never did.

Friday nights we were allowed to stay up late and watch Hawaii Five-0, The Tommy Hunter Show, and Carol Burnett. There would be one bag of Humpty Dumpty potato chips and one big bottle of Pop Shoppe pop for all of us to share. It was divided equally until none was left and no one complained. We also had one bathroom to share and this was a challenge when you desperately needed to go. Wanda made up a pee dance based on one of Carol Burnett's characters. Whenever the character walked, the drum made a *sa sum sa sum sum* sound. So every time we were waiting in line for the bathroom, we stood outside the door laughing, with a tea towel wrapped around our neck (not sure what significance this held!), and danced around singing *sa sum sa sum sum*. This both killed time and helped with the pee holding process. It was also hilarious.

Wanda was also very creative with language and would make up words. Being a younger naive sister who looked up to her, I thought the words were real. Try Googling the word "diggy" and you won't find the way we used it. To us, it meant when someone was kind of nerdy and wore untrendy clothes. An example of this in a sentence is, "Oh just look at his pants. How diggy."

A typical Christmas morning would start with a Bible reading about Jesus' birth, singing around the piano, and then opening gifts. Our stockings would contain an orange, nuts, and old fashioned Christmas candy. The candy was loose in the stocking so it stuck to everything, including the nuts. Mom wasn't great at packing stockings, but she was quite practical when buying presents, which was better than nothing since Santa never visited our house. She would mostly give necessities like socks, pyjamas, and clothes. A new game for everyone might be under the tree, so we girls would open that one together. Payday was one of my favourites but we also had Monopoly. It seemed like that game went on forever even though we never incorporated the hotels and houses. I guess we just weren't inquisitive enough to use them and were satisfied with our simple gameplay.

Later on Christmas Day, we would head out to one of the Meadows' homes. During these visits, it would strike me just how poor we were. Our cousins would have the latest toys, including new dolls that walked and talked. I genuinely struggled to answer questions about my gifts because the ones I got could never compare with theirs. I never wanted to be rude, so I would honestly and humbly explain the meagre gifts I had received.

Aside from the gifts, food and family were the main focus at the Meadows' family Christmas. My mom's family always made us feel welcome with plenty of hugs, kisses, and laughter. After we got home, we would discuss our day with Mom. Later in bed, me and my sisters would share our deepest thoughts and feelings, each taking a turn empathizing with one another. This connected us and affirmed our feelings. My heart and my head would be clear of all negative thoughts and emotions allowing me to feel content and fall asleep.

My sisters and I were there for each other. We helped one another overcome challenges any way we could. Our mother really loved playing the piano, and every time we needed her she seemed too busy practicing. Maybe not having a father made us tougher and more independent, but whatever the reason, we all were there for each other, especially Wanda and I.

Wanda came to my rescue and helped me get to the doctor's office, just down the street, when I needed a thorn removed from the top of my head. I had been running around in a wooded area overgrown with thorn trees at the end of our road. Our doctor first froze around the thorn, and then used the end of the needle to pry it out.

I helped Wanda another time when I pulled a nail out of her foot. The nail was sticking up from a piece of wood and she had accidentally stepped on it. She was crying her head off and couldn't calm down. I calmly said, "Give me your foot," braced it between my knees, and yanked the nail out. I just wanted the crying to stop.

I wasn't keen on public shows of vulnerability and also hated seeing people in pain. I cried in private but tried not to in public. Wanda, on the other hand, would cry quite openly and Linda was somewhere in the middle of us two. I always thought crying showed weakness, so you shouldn't do it. Plus Mom also discouraged us from crying, saying things like, "Oh, you're fine. Stop that crying."

First fatherless, then penniless, and next godliness. Will this all work together or against me?

Mom and us three girls at church.
Left to right - Me, Linda, and Wanda

CHAPTER SIX

RELIGION RULES

1968-1974

As an avid member of the Pentecostal Church in Arkona, my mom was determined to uphold her convictions and to make us girls accountable. We grew up attending church twice on Sunday: once in the morning, including Sunday School, and then at night after supper. We usually had time to watch Wonderful World of Disney before heading out in the evening. In addition to Sunday, there were prayer meetings, tent meetings, Vacation Bible School, church camp, and youth groups.

In conjunction with all these church activities was Mom's own set of rules. As young girls, we weren't allowed to wear make-up or earrings, go to the movies, or even dance. Gym classes used to incorporate dance lessons as part of the curriculum, but Mom wrote a note excusing us. I remember sitting on the bench, bored and embarrassed, watching my peers spinning each other around.

When we reached adolescence, Mom did concede on a few of the restrictions and allowed us to wear make-up and get our ears pierced. Dancing and going to movies remained out of bounds, but as young teens, we just rebelled and did what we wanted. We felt being grounded for a week was worth the trade-off. There was never a drop of alcohol (unless we snuck it in), cursing (especially using the Lord's name in vain), smoking cigarettes, or a single deck of playing cards allowed in our house. But I grew up in a community where drugs were readily available, so along with alcohol and smoking, I experimented. It all just seemed a part of growing up in Arkona and helped me cope with the boredom and angst that came with being a teenager.

For my mom, Christmas was for celebrating the birth of Jesus—there was no such thing as Santa in our house. On the list of "no shows" to our home were: the Easter Bunny, the Tooth Fairy, leprechauns, princes and princesses, godmothers; well, you get the picture. Fantasy worlds were omitted from our childhood. Bible stories and Bible readings were the truth as Mom felt it necessary to carry out her duties as a Bible-believing Christian. Those were the only types of reading materials found in our home. By the time I was a teenager, I was convinced my mom had robbed me of my childhood. I vowed to raise my kids differently if I were to be blessed with them.

When I was a child, I spent the weekends at the three ladies' house whenever I had trouble coping with Mom's strict ways. I would call them up and ask for a sleepover, and if they weren't busy, away I went. They knew I needed a break from home and would spoil me with affection, activities, and attention. Little did I know then what a big part of my life they would always be. They were just like having another three moms only they offered me much more than the physical support my mother gave. Their kind gentle ways, listening ears, and supportive words gave me an emotional boost, essential to a young deserving child, especially one as shy as I was. I would then return home prepared and renewed emotionally, ready to face the coming week at school.

CHAPTER SEVEN

SHY LITTLE REDHEAD

1975-1977

You would think with the absence of funds we couldn't afford piano lessons or summer camp. However, our church sponsored us so we could go to church camp in Paris, Ontario, every summer. Wanda and Linda had friends to take, our cousins mainly, but I felt like a fifth wheel. This should have forced me to make friends of my own, but I remained shy and stubborn. It was hard for me to even start a conversation with my peers. Children my age, at times, seemed so immature I wondered what we would even have in common. There was a girl my age, living in Arkona, who wanted to hang out. Her laugh was unique, but I thought it sounded silly and ridiculous. I felt she was doing it for attention, so I made up excuses not to hang out anymore. I was too picky, as there weren't many girls my age in Arkona. As a result, I ended up with very few friends.

I also had the privilege to take piano (Grandma Meadows called it a "pie-anna") lessons until I was sixteen years old. Mom must have scrimped and saved to afford these lessons. Over a ten year period, I had three female teachers. Their ages varied from elderly, middle-aged, to just a few years older than me. At the time, I was rebellious and said, "I'm not taking them anymore. I hate playing the piano." What did I really mean? I didn't like playing Conservatory music anymore and would soon have to start playing at recitals to pass into the next grade of piano. Being shy, self-conscious, and insecure, that just wasn't an option for me. I was too scared and didn't see any real future for me in piano. Being able to read the notes and getting up to grade six, though, helped me through music in high school. All I had to do was learn how to play the flute. Once I had mastered the proper breathing technique and finger placement, the rest came easily.

Along with my red hair came curls and waves. Most women would die for these characteristics, but as a young girl, it seemed more like a curse than a blessing. And no doubt being different added to my shyness. What I didn't know then was that you shouldn't brush or comb your hair once it's dry, so my hair always seemed uncontrollable. Mom took care of that by having the hairdresser chop it off into a Pixie cut, leaving me looking like a boy.

This was confirmed one summer while riding around in my grandparents' taxi. Grandma Hawkins drove the taxi for her and Grandpa's business. Part of their day included picking up and dropping off the mail carriers for the City of Strathroy. One of the mailmen she transported commented on how cute her grandson was while glancing my way. I was mortified. I cried every time during the dreaded walk to the hairdressers. I'm sure they felt sorry for me and tried to make light of the situation, but they had been instructed by my mom to lop it off. I'm still not a fan of going to the beauty salon and like wearing my hair long. Luckily it has maintained enough colour and curl, so I don't perm or dye it. I only need a couple of visits per year. I love being a redhead now. It only took me fifty years!

Even though I was shy, athletics and elementary school classwork came easily for me. But a few more hurtful nicknames and phrases were added to the repertoire by my peers. Ones like "Fireball 500" (not sure if it was after a fast race car or after my red hair) and "The redhead is dead." That last one could easily have been misinterpreted as a threat. Probably if I hadn't reacted and just played along and laughed my tormentors would have stopped. But that was impossible for me to do so the bullies got what they wanted ... a target.

I enjoyed most sports, and was on the volleyball team and looked forward to track and field, intramural sports, and running around outside. I was a people pleaser, so teachers found me to be a shy, quiet, and willing learner—although comments on my report cards claimed I was chatty at the wrong times. Overall, though, I prided myself on my good grades. Being intelligent and athletic gave me the self-confidence to perform well academically and physically. Socially, however, I lacked the skills required to make and maintain friendships. I was always so serious, and my work had to be done to perfection or not at all. Even though I was shy and insecure about my looks, especially my white skin, freckles, and red hair, my success at athletics and academics was enough to carry me through. I finished grade eight strong-willed and eager for secondary school.

CHAPTER EIGHT

CHOOSING A PATH

1978-1985

"Hi, Wendy. I heard you had an awesome year at the elementary track and field meet. We'd love for you to join our team here at NLSS. What do you think?" asked the female high school coach.

"Thank you, but I'm honestly not interested," I replied. As I walked away, I felt waves of disappointment.

"Well, if you change your mind … " she called after me.

Why didn't I just tell her the truth? I had avoided phys ed classes once I heard you had to shower with other girls. My self-consciousness led to this choice, but I wish I had been open to exploring options. Things back then, to me, seemed cut-and-dried thanks to the tunnel vision I'd inherited from my mom. We didn't explore every opportunity but rather accepted things and didn't think outside the box. We thought in black and white, not colour. Maybe I could have been excused from showering, or there could have been separate stalls where I wouldn't have to be nude in front of others. I never even thought to find out.

Getting good grades in high school did not come as easily to me as it did in elementary school. This is when my mental and social health started spiralling downward. Anxiety, worry, and self-doubt caused me to struggle with daily life. I smoked to be cool, drank alcohol to be brave, and eliminated sports from my life to avoid showering in public.

My first boyfriend came along when I was fifteen, and I fell head over heels. Not having parents to role model a loving relationship, I struggled with what a healthy relationship should look like. Things didn't go well between me and my boyfriend. I felt hopeless and defeated, and decided to take an overdose of aspirins to help numb the pain and possibly end my life. This resulted in a visit to the hospital and a psychiatrist. Both left me feeling guilty and ashamed, so I didn't see it as an opportunity for healing and recovery. Instead, I was left wondering what was wrong with me.

Oddly enough, caring for others contributed to my recovery. Babysitting was one area where I felt needed so it became a priority. Also, I needed the money for my list of growing vices. Aside from the cash, I enjoyed working with the children. In their eyes, I could do no wrong.

Their friendship and love was unconditional. I continued caring for children most of my teen years. I even had a live-in nanny and housekeeper position for one summer on a fruit farm outside of Arkona. I was responsible for the cooking, cleaning, laundry, and childcare duties. They felt I was mature enough to drive their car, so I even took the kids to the beach. The family constantly praised my work ethic and childcare skills, and I finally started to gain some self-worth.

The following summer Mom and I were having frequent disputes about her inflexible rules so I jumped at an opportunity to visit my friend, Suzie, in Stratford. We met a few years earlier when her family was living in Arkona but then lost touch. While visiting her uncle in Arkona that summer we reconnected and I found out she had quit high school and was working at a factory. She claimed that she loved working and earning money and encouraged me to do the same. Her parents were even willing to let me board at their house. It all seemed so easy.

Mom allowed me to go there under the following condition: if I didn't find a job and returned home, I had to finish high school. I went there with the hopes of becoming a live-in nanny now that I had considerable childcare experience and had enjoyed it so much. If I were to land a suitable job, I was fully prepared to quit school, at sixteen years of age, and stay in Stratford. I registered with the employment office and waited for the jobs to pour in.

In the meantime, Suzie and her parents went to work during the day, so I stayed home and helped out in any way I could. One day I was left in charge of turning on the supper. You'd think this would be easy enough for a stellar housekeeper. Both of her parents were deaf and instead of telling me the instructions her mother left a note outlining the time the roast should be turned on and the temperature it needed to cook at. I did as asked but when they returned home there was some confusion and much laughter. I was supposed to turn on the electric frying pan but had thought they meant the oven. I didn't have the common sense to check if the roast was actually in the oven when I turned it on. Luckily for me, they were good sports and teased me in their special way. As fate would have it, no job ever surfaced and I returned home after a couple of weeks.

Being a nanny was an attainable goal for me as it didn't require post secondary education and I had already proven myself capable in that particular role. But since that idea didn't pan out, I was forced to finish high school as agreed upon. In the fall, I returned to school and completed secondary school with business subjects as my major focus. Since we had to follow some sort of career path while in high school, my dream job was to work as a secretary, but I knew that meant more education and more money. So I never considered this an attainable goal. My typing speed was above average and I had completed all the courses (except shorthand which I had dropped during a teacher strike) required to begin a secretarial or business diploma at college.

College didn't happen for me due to financial constraints—remember, we were living on government assistance. Borrowing money for education was never a viable option. It seemed like an option for other people, not for us poor families. So I went right out of high school to a laborious, dirty, factory job in Watford, Ontario. A few years later, I took a lay-off at the factory with the hopes of gaining more meaningful employment. I lived on unemployment insurance benefits and supplemented my income with a part-time job as a waitress at a small restaurant. By then, I was living on my own in an apartment in Watford. I lived paycheque to paycheque, barely making ends meet. I had purchased a car before leaving home, and had the pleasure of maintaining that money pit.

Just before my unemployment insurance claim terminated, I was accepted into a new government initiative called O.C.A.P. (the Ontario Career Action Program). My placement was at an employment insurance office in Strathroy, where I acquired some office skills like typing, filing, and data input. After the O.C.A.P finished, I was hired at a home improvement and lumber company where I worked in a small office. I would take orders over the phone, write them down, and then the yard manager would assemble the loads for the outgoing trucks. Another part of my job was to call railroad companies to pick up their empty railroad cars. I found this part the most interesting.

My knowledge of lumber and home improvement was limited, so it was difficult transcribing the information when I didn't even know what the materials were. Many times, I would have to ask the caller how to spell the item. Luckily for me, I had very patient co-workers. I asked the yard manager to take me on a tour of the warehouse to get a better understanding of their inventory. This helped me somewhat, but seeing how the materials were actually used would have been more beneficial. This job unquestionably wasn't my thing, but I needed the money so I stuck it out.

With all the struggles I was having on the work front, I set my sights on finding a husband and having children. I had long wanted to create the "normal" family I had lacked as a child. Little did I know at the time that having children of my own would not be as easy as I thought.

CHAPTER NINE

SETTLING DOWN

1985

Eighteen years after my father died, my mother and I both set out to find love and settle down. Mom would often say, "Who needs a man anyway," or "Men are trouble," so it shocked me when I found out she was interested in dating the new pastor at the Arkona Baptist Church. She was a changed person—besotted, giddy, and lovestruck. I loved this new side of her, but I was also worried. What if her feelings were not reciprocated by Michael Liew and she was hurt and disillusioned? Would this cause her to fall again into depression? Since Michael had never married or had children of his own, Mom entertained the idea of having a child with him if they married. I thought she was far too old for this and should put this preposterous idea behind her and look forward to having grandchildren.

Being a pastor's wife had been Mom's dream, and in October of 1985 her dream was fulfilled. She married Michael in the presence of two witnesses, friends of theirs at the time. Her prayers had been answered. God had brought her a man all the way from Malaysia. A good man, just right for her. Unfortunately for Michael, Mom was beginning her menopausal years so she couldn't have any more children.

Around the same time Mom found love, so did I. This was no easy task, as my mother had not dated many men while raising me. It was difficult for me to imagine a loving relationship between a man and a woman. Sure, there were my grandparents, aunts and uncles, and friends' parents to watch, but unless you have lived in that type of environment, it's a totally foreign concept. And it didn't help that Mom fixated on me marrying a preacher and having a big family. That was her dream, not mine. Thankfully, my headstrong nature helped me stay true to myself.

At the beginning of 1985, I met Jim Scott on a blind date and fell hopelessly in love. I was working for the lumber company and living in Watford with my sister Linda. He was living in Point Edward, Ontario and working in Sarnia, Ontario for a high-pressure water company. I loved everything about him, including his very good looks, physique, decisiveness, take-charge personality, and, of course, his blue Camaro.

For one of our first dates he took me fishing. Afterwards,

he built a fire and whipped up a supper of steak and baked potatoes on a grill. He just happened to have the grill in his trunk. This undeniably impressed me. And for the first time in my life, I felt special and loved by a man.

Our relationship progressed extremely fast. Within six months, I was pregnant. The baby was due around March of 1986. I honestly thought you couldn't conceive that fast. I found out I was pregnant while visiting the doctor to get birth control pills. Before that, I had applied to Lambton College for the Early Childhood Education program and had been accepted. Once I found out about the baby, I left the program. It didn't even cross my mind to think outside the box and try to manage both school and the pregnancy.

In the fall, I found myself wondering where I'd live. Linda and I were roomies, but she had decided to attend a Bible College in Whitby, Ontario. I couldn't afford the apartment we had been sharing on my own, so Jim and I decided to move in together. We agreed it was best for us financially and, of course, with the baby on the way it only made sense. Earlier in the year, Jim had moved from Point Edward to Inwood, Ontario to be closer to me and his family and away from the city. He was renting a house from his brother and I moved in with him.

We lived there until January of 1986, and then we bought a house together that was too good of a deal to pass up. We paid twenty thousand dollars for our first home and all it needed was a bathroom renovation. The rest of the house was fine.

I quit working at the lumber yard after Jim and I decided it was unsafe for me to navigate the unpredictable winter weather and road conditions while pregnant. This left me plenty of time to set up the nursery and create the perfect, loving nest for when the baby came. I had learned how to crochet and knit as a young girl, so I lovingly spent hours making a yellow baby blanket, and carefully placed it over the edge of the cradle. All the room really needed was a baby to bring it to life. Jim's family quickly became a big part of my life after they welcomed me with open arms. My relationship with Jim blossomed from all the support we received from our families and the love we had for each other. Our home and hearts were ready to welcome a new member to our family.

Life was never more perfect. Then the unthinkable happened.

CHAPTER TEN

A TIME OF LOVE
AND LOSS

January 31, 1986

"Wendy, I can't find a heartbeat." It was a cold winter day in January when the on-call doctor revealed this heart-wrenching news to Jim and me. I had been busy cleaning and arranging the cupboards in our first home in the metropolis of Inwood (really, hamlet is a better descriptor since it was even smaller than Arkona). I was seven and a half months pregnant and the pregnancy had been progressing pretty normally. I had experienced a little bit of spotting a month earlier, but the doctor had simply recommended bed rest for a few days. That respite seemed to ease my symptoms so I returned to my normal routine. I hadn't stopped smoking, but I had discussed the pros and cons with my doctor, friends, and family. They all said to cut back, and my mother mentioned she had smoked while pregnant. Stats back then indicated you would just have a smaller baby.

I was standing at the kitchen sink doing dishes when suddenly I felt a gush between my legs. Looking down at the beige kitchen mat, I saw blood starting to run over the sides and onto the floor. I ran to the bathroom, pulled down my pants and underwear, and watched in a paralyzed panic as blood gushed into the toilet. It kept filling the bowl and I kept flushing. It just wouldn't stop. How could this be happening?

I quickly realized I had to get to the nearest hospital. With a towel between my legs, I rushed to the phone and dialled my sister-in-law, Julie, next door. Jim was there visiting. He rushed home to drive me to the hospital in Petrolia. Upon arrival, I was whisked to the first available room where the doctor examined me, hoping to find the baby's heartbeat. Nothing. "Maybe the baby is just turned away and he isn't trying hard enough," I thought. This can't be happening.

A specialist was called in. The news wasn't good. The baby was deceased and would have to be delivered. At that point, delivering my baby vaginally just didn't seem real or normal. "Can't they do a C-section and take the baby out?" I asked. Nope. "We are going to wait and see if it proceeds on its own," they said.

The doctors knew my baby was dead. This allowed for drugs to be used to alleviate my pain since it couldn't have negative effects on the baby. It did, however, have negative effects on me. I was exhausted and couldn't keep my eyes open. In between sleeping and waking, I felt nauseous and sometimes threw up. I was thankful when sleep took me, as it was better than feeling scared, anxious, and numb. No doubt the blood loss and drugs didn't help. Jim and his dad sat patiently waiting for something to happen, comforting me and each other. I curled up and held it all in, hoping it would all be over soon.

Being in a hazy fog, I don't remember how long it took. Time stood still. Eventually, though, later that night, it did happen on its own. I pushed and before long the stillborn baby was delivered. No tears of joy, only sorrow. No newborn baby cry. Just silence.

Jim was allowed into the delivery room afterwards and we spent a few moments with our son. There, in that cold sterile atmosphere, would be our only chance to see him. He looked perfect—like a little sleeping angel. Oh, how I long to recall every detail of him, but I can't. If words were spoken I don't remember them either. All I wanted to do was sleep peacefully with my son in my arms.

The next day brought new developments. After losing so much blood I was extremely pale, weak, and tired so the nurses called in the doctor. They determined I needed several blood transfusions. In the early eighties, there was a significant risk of receiving blood tainted with HIV or Hepatitis C. I didn't realize I was taking chances with what was likely unscreened blood, but thankfully things turned out fine and that burden wasn't added to having a stillbirth.

We all tried to make sense of the terrible loss in our own way and to find some closure while in the throes of grief and sorrow. Jim released his emotions by constantly crying, whereas I buried my emotions so I didn't have to deal with them.

My sister-in-law Diane was a nurse at the hospital and happened to be on shift at the time. Much later she shared with me that when she saw my son she had said, "He's like a beautiful little angel gone to heaven," and all the staff agreed. My sister-in-law Barb offered heartfelt words and hours of consolation. When Barb explained, "He was too good for this world, Wendy," I grabbed onto that and held tight. It was the only explanation that made sense, and I hoped God had spared my son a struggle down here on earth.

Alaric Leonard Scott was named after Dad as I didn't have the chance to get to know either of them. He was buried on top of my Dad instead of with the other deceased children in the cemetery. Mom had contacted Dad's parents about Alaric's death and they offered the gravesite. Alaric's final resting place was appropriate given our circumstance. We had just purchased our home that month, so money was tight. And I found some comfort in knowing neither my dad nor Alaric would be alone. I believe all we paid for was the small coffin and burial fees.

The doctor said I was too weak to attend the funeral, so I slept and secretly wept. Jim, and both our families, went to the gravesite and my stepdad, Michael, delivered the Bible reading from Ecclesiastes.

Ecclesiastes 3:1-8, King James Version
To every thing there is a season,
and a time to every purpose under the heaven:
A time to be born, a time to die;
a time to plant, and a time to pluck
up that which is planted;
A time to kill, and a time to heal;
a time to break down, and a time to build up;
A time to weep, and a time to laugh;
a time to mourn, and a time to dance;
A time to cast away stones, and a
time to gather stones together;
a time to embrace, and a time to
refrain from embracing;
A time to get, and a time to lose;
a time to keep, and a time to cast away;
A time to rend, and a time to sew;
a time to keep silence, and a time to speak;
A time to love, and a time to hate;
A time of war, and a time of peace.

I'm sure there wasn't a dry eye after that scripture was read. And many were asking God, "Why did you let this happen?" Regrets surrounding the death of my son followed me for many years. I shouldn't have smoked during my pregnancy or had premarital sex. I also wished I had pictures of Alaric so I could remember what he looked like.

At this time in my life I wasn't attending church, but believing in Heaven helped bring some peace to my shattered world. I envisioned my son in a wonderful place with no pain or suffering, just happiness. I prayed for forgiveness to free me from my pain and guilt. I wondered, "Would I be forgiven and granted the gift of a healthy baby?" If you have ever loved and lost, then you will understand exactly how I was feeling following the loss of my child. All the hopes and dreams for your life together must be forgotten. My blood-stained clothes, towel, and mat were destroyed and the nursery was dismantled. Crib, clothes, and toys were tucked away in the closet, but my fears, guilt, and sadness remained.

"You'll have another baby," is the worst thing you can say to a mother who has lost a child. How does that help? To start with it suggests the baby who died is easily replaced. I guess some people think it gives the mother hope to try again, but I was terrified to have another baby. I was producing breast milk and had no baby to feed. Pills were prescribed and it dried it up. All the blood loss was constantly on my mind, not to mention how weak I felt. Iron pills eventually brought my levels back up, but nothing helped with my worry, guilt, melancholy, hopelessness, and insomnia.

Eventually, I was diagnosed with depression and prescribed an antidepressant. I was reluctant to take medication, but I gave in as I was determined to feel better. After several months, things didn't look so gray. I felt like I had a life worth living. Instead of sinking deeper and deeper into the abyss, I gradually swam to the top. At times, it felt like I was being held under water again, but one walk, talk, or outing later and I rose above those murky waters.

It was during this time of loss we were hit with yet another devastating blow. This time it was Jim's turn.

CHAPTER ELEVEN

THE FALL

1986 - Spring

The beginning of 1986 had proven to be quite eventful with the purchase of our first home and then the loss of our baby. We were barely coping when yet another major incident dropped on us. But before I continue with that story, I want to share something good that happened. Sometimes it's nice to pepper the bad with the good.

Shortly after our loss, Jim realized how lonely I was, especially while he was at work. His shifts were inconsistent and involved many evenings and nights away from home. One day, while I was slumped on the couch, he appeared with an adorable, fluffy, gray kitten. It was still too young to be permanently away from its mother but would be ready to join our family in a few weeks. I couldn't resist petting his soft fur, cuddling his warm body, and listening to his gentle, incessant purring. I fell in love with him instantly and I told Jim we needed him.

Two weeks later, he returned and remained with me for fifteen years. We named him Sambo. He became our fierce hunter, night prowler, playful pal, and dependable cuddler. After looking both ways, he'd cross the road in front of our house to hunt in the deep, cattail-filled ditch. He was like a dog and always came when I yelled out the backdoor, "Sambo. Here Sambo." He would magically appear from under the neighbour's shed door, where he spent the remainder of his nights after his hunt was over.

Sambo was friendly and outgoing for the most part, but he sometimes acted aloof. You might try to call him to you for a cuddle, but he would just walk on by. He was a typical cat and we loved him. I talked to Sambo many nights while Jim was away at work and he helped comfort me through my loss, just by being there. He was a really good listener.

March 22, 1986

Now back to the bad—an accident happened at Jim's workplace that would affect him for the rest of his life. Being a lanceman, his job required him to work with high-pressure water and this could be dangerous if you didn't have your wits about you. Since the water was used to cut materials such as rubber or cement, it could have severe effects on a human body if safety precautions were not correctly followed.

One night, Jim was leaning up against a metal railing to give himself the leverage needed to complete a job. The metal railing gave out, causing him to fall back onto it. Luckily, once his foot left the pedal controlling the water pressure the lance was disabled. But his lower back was severely injured from the fall onto the railing, and he was treated similarly to someone with a spinal fracture.

Jim endured a tremendous amount of pain while different treatment options were discussed. Pain medication, traction, and bed rest were prescribed, but it wasn't until chiropractic treatments were incorporated that he could tolerate riding in a vehicle. Surgery was discussed with his doctor, but after careful consideration of the complications and risks he declined.

While coping with Jim's injury, the bills didn't stop coming in. I was entitled to maternity benefits even though I had lost my child. We were thankful for this income while we anticipated Jim's recovery and the uncertainty surrounding his physical abilities for future opportunites with his employer.

Meanwhile, my prayer list was growing. Each night I asked Jesus to lay his healing hands upon Jim and me and make us happy and whole. I questioned why all these challenges were happening to us and if our choice to remain living together, unmarried, had caused our misfortune. Guilt over our living arrangement and smoking during my pregnancy played a huge role in my lengthy recovery.

In the early days following Jim's injury, it was tough to see him in so much pain. I woke up each morning feeling nauseous but didn't know why. Sometimes I felt like crawling back in bed with him and laying there all day too. But, I forced myself out of bed and faced the day, since meals still had to be cooked and daily chores completed. At least being Jim's caregiver afforded me a sense of purpose and I turned my focus on him instead of myself.

Slowly, we started becoming stronger, both physically and mentally. We faced each day with the renewed hope that things were going to get better and reminded each other that if we got through this, we could get through anything! The unexpected gift of time together allowed us to reflect on what we still had to look forward to. My doctor said there was no reason we couldn't try to have another baby, and Jim's doctor had hope he would be able to return to work soon. We demonstrated that we could remain together for better or for worse and in sickness and in health. After 1986 was well behind us, we forged ahead with the next step in our relationship.

CHAPTER TWELVE

MARRIAGE BEFORE CARRIAGE

August 29, 1987

The topic of marriage had first come up between Jim and me when I was pregnant with Alaric. I declined. I didn't want to feel like we **had** to get married. But with our loss behind us, it was time to officially devote our lives to each other.

Even though Jim was recovered and back to work, we were still a one-income family and had purchased a new vehicle and house the previous year. So we kept our wedding extremely simple. Wanda and Linda insisted on being a part of my wedding day. I accepted their offers to do my hair and makeup and I felt beautiful. Our small wedding was held at a little Baptist church outside of Inwood, and the only people in attendance other than the bride and groom were two witnesses (Jim's sister and brother-in-law), a minister, and a photographer. Afterwards, we took our attendants out for lunch and then headed to Niagara Falls, Ontario, for our honeymoon.

Many years later, I regretted not having my family at the church that day. It just didn't seem possible, at the time, for this to happen. We lacked the funds for a bigger wedding, so we settled for the bare minimum.

The actual ceremony, I had thought, would certainly make it right with God instead of continuing to live common law. It also fulfilled one of my dreams of having a husband. Now all that was left was having children.

Before I would allow myself to become pregnant again, I vowed to quit smoking. Jim quit first to prove to me it was possible. He appeared to quit effortlessly, whereas I found it very difficult. We both quit cold turkey, but we were two different people approaching the situation from our perspectives and with differing levels of will power.

Chewing lots of gum, walking, and knitting kept me busy enough to finally overcome the awful habit. It took months for the nicotine cravings to subside, but I was amazed at how much better food tasted and how wonderful the world smelled. This led to some weight gain but I quickly nipped that in the bud by cutting back, eating healthier, and being more active. Although I finally felt free of the "monkey on my back," it occasionally would haunt my dreams. I used to startle awake thinking I had started smoking again. It would take me a few minutes to realize it was just a bad dream. After waiting a few years to recover and repair the damage caused by smoking, I felt confident and ready to try for another baby.

In the meantime, with my health and self confidence growing stronger, I accepted a permanent occasional clerk position at Brooke Municipal Telephone. I assisted with billing and filled in for office staff when they went on vacation. The office was close enough to home that I could walk or ride my bike. And the job had potential for advancement. Things were looking up.

CHAPTER THIRTEEN

A BIG ADDITION

1989-1990

Of course I wanted to be the perfect parent. On top of reading a lot of parent magazines and library books, I insisted we use condoms for a couple of menstrual cycles after I quit birth control pills to ensure any medication was out of my system before getting pregnant. We didn't have to wait long. My family doctor and I agreed I should be under a specialist's care, so I was referred back to the doctor previously called in to assist with my stillborn. He was older and experienced and I trusted him completely. Ultrasounds became routine due to my history, along with any other tests he could think of. He wasn't taking any chances and ran me through the gamut.

This pregnancy felt good and right but the fear of losing another baby was on my mind, particularly up to the seven-and-a-half month mark. That's when I had lost Alaric. As that milestone approached, I just tried to relax. I had done everything I could, including exercising, praying, eating healthy, and taking prenatal vitamins. I also avoided other medications and had quit smoking and drinking. I was also cognizant of if my baby was moving regularly. This was something that hadn't even been discussed with Alaric. Sure, there were times while standing at the kitchen sink when I'd flashback to that fateful day I lost Alaric. During those moments, I would pray for strength and courage. And remind myself getting upset would not be good for me or the baby. The fear would eventually pass and I could continue with my day.

Two weeks before my projected delivery date I stopped by the doctor's office for a routine check up. During my pelvic examination, the doctor said, "You are dilated enough to deliver this baby. I'm guessing given how much weight you've gained it'll be over ten pounds. Everything is going well, but based on your previous history I don't want to take any chances. Do you want to have your baby today?"

I was shocked. I hadn't realized doctors could arrange when a baby is to be born unless it was by C-section. Of course, I trusted his judgement, "I'm ready. What do I need to do?"

Jim and I headed to St. Joseph's hospital in Sarnia later that day, ready to meet our baby. I was settled into a room and prepared for the upcoming delivery. After the doctor broke my water things progressed as expected. After lots and lots and lots of pushing, Darian James Scott was born on March 16, 1990, weighing 9 lbs. 12 oz. He was a very healthy, alert, and big baby … especially for a woman who is only 5' 3".

We were ecstatic and I had never seen Jim more proud. He had genuinely wanted our firstborn to be a boy. Our hospital stay was a little longer than normal, as Darian developed jaundice. Since I was nursing, I stayed as well. After phototherapy treatment, which involved placing him under a blue light for a few days, we were finally given the okay to go home.

Bringing Darian home terrified me. The world around us was moving so fast and cars whizzed by. I didn't want anything to happen to him. I just wanted to get home where we would all be safe. The drive home from Sarnia seemed to take forever. In reality, it would have taken only about thirty-five minutes.

Having a huge newborn was really like having a month-old baby. He only wore newborn sizes for about a week before I had to switch his wardrobe for the next size up. It was a blessing that Darian immediately slept through the night (well, at least six hours straight through), so we never had to experience all those sleepless nights everyone warns about. Darian was passive, content, and nursed well. I remember Jim putting baby oil in his light brown hair to make it appear darker like his. Later on, as a young child, his hair turned quite blonde, but it eventually changed to his current colour of dark brown. I was just thankful it wasn't red. Boys with red hair never appealed to me and I didn't want him to endure the same teasing I had experienced as a child.

We were proud of our good fortune and ecstatic with our perfect child. So much so we decided to have another baby. The thought never crossed our minds that we could encounter more obstacles while trying to grow our family.

CHAPTER FOURTEEN

UNBEARABLE PAIN

February 12, 1993

"Mrs. Scott, your baby has been absorbed by your body," said the ultrasound technician. I was writhing in pain and couldn't comprehend what that meant.

We had decided to try for another child since Darian was doing so well and we had always wanted two children. I had read in several parent magazines how a two-to three-year span between children is an ideal timeframe because it gives you lots of time with the first child before the second one becomes the centre of attention. According to the research, we were right on target.

A few short months after using no contraception, I was pregnant. This was confirmed through blood, urine, and ultrasound testing. My family doctor always erred on the side of caution, knowing my history. An ultrasound wasn't a routine procedure for most women, but it was for me.

"This time it'll be like my last pregnancy with Darian. Everything is going to be fine," I thought. I had been through too much already. God would not let anything else bad happen to me.

Weeks later, I was in unbearable pain—pain worse than labour—and had another ultrasound to see what was going on. I am still surprised the technician told me my baby had been absorbed. I'm pretty sure they aren't supposed to interpret and share test results. I was relieved when my family doctor suggested they call in the Ob/Gyn specialist who assisted with the stillbirth. After examining me, he diagnosed me as having an ectopic, or tubal, pregnancy. I needed emergency surgery or I could die if the fallopian tube ruptured. Once again, I was wheeled into an operating room in disbelief. But I trusted my Ob/Gyn and felt quite confident he was capable of handling my situation. The constant pain consumed my every thought until I finally slipped into oblivion thanks to the anesthesia.

I awoke to find my abdomen covered with a very wide bandage. I didn't want to know what had happened under there. I soon learned the doctors first tried using a scope to be less intrusive but had to resort to the full surgical procedure where they make a large incision along your bikini line, remove the tubal pregnancy, and then close the wound with staples. Not pretty, but as far as I was concerned they had saved my life once again. Who knew having kids was going to be this hard?

The surgeon explained the procedure had gone well and that there was no reason why I shouldn't be able to conceive again. I asked if he had ever come across another patient like me who had a stillborn, a healthy baby, and then an ectopic pregnancy. He said, "No Wendy, I haven't encountered this in all my years of practice. I've had patients who have miscarried, but not one with your exact circumstances." After hearing that, I felt unique but at the same time wondered, "What else could go wrong?"

Again I was left feeling the loss of another baby, but I felt fortunate to have Darian. As I told friends and family about my struggles, I discovered many women I knew had experienced similar losses and could empathize. Most of the women did not feel comfortable talking about their loss unless I asked them to. Learning I was not alone gave me some comfort and taught me that bad things do happen to good people. It also gave me the extra hope I needed to recover, as all of the women had overcome their setbacks and continued to grow their families. Time heals everything. My incision slowly healed, as did my disappointment. I thanked Jesus for my health, husband, son, family, and friends. Of course I prayed to be blessed with another child, but I also wondered if it would be morally right to continue trying in fear I'd end up with another dead baby. And in the back of my mind, I slowly started to think about if there was another way to grow my family.

PART TWO

THE SEARCH

CHAPTER FIFTEEN

A FOUNT OF KNOWLEDGE

1993

In Part One, I offered the reader a sweeping story of love and loss. From the death of my father, to my childhood and family relationships, to my long, painful journey to grow my family, you got a glimpse into the beautiful highs and heartbreaking lows that made me a tenacious, inquisitive, and empathetic person—a person ready for the next chapter in her life: the search.

After I recovered from my ectopic pregnancy, we tried to get pregnant for quite a while. It was during this time I got to thinking that I may not be able to have another child. This would mean no brother or sister for Darian. Would he be lonely? I also started thinking about my half-brother or half-sister and how they must feel being an only child. I knew for a fact my Dad and the young girl he had been with only had one child together and my mom always assumed it was put up for adoption. I supposed they could have siblings at their adoptive home, but they wouldn't be blood relatives like me and my sisters. I wondered if my half-sibling ever felt alone. Would they want to know their family history?

I decided to get serious about finding my half-sibling. I contacted my mom and began to question her. At first she challenged me. She asked, "Why do you want to do that?" I answered, "Because this person is my brother or sister and I feel it's something I am led to do. I need closure. I want them to know about me, to know that I want to get to know them. Who knows? Maybe we can even build a relationship." After this exchange, she gave me all the information she knew about the child. It wasn't much, but she did direct me to Aunt Myrna. Deep down, I may have been asking Mom's permission, but I knew her well enough to know she wasn't going to be totally okay with my plan. But this was something I had to do, regardless.

My dad's family, the Hawkinses, were always so kind and made my mom, sisters, and I feel like we were a part of their family. Christmases in Strathroy and summer holidays at the cottage in Ipperwash became a tradition. So Wanda, Linda, and I were close to our grandparents, aunts, uncles, and cousins. I have very fond memories of spending time with the Hawkinses. Grandma would let us dress up in her high heels and earrings, carry her purses, and strut down the streets of Strathroy. The sock monkey and string of wooden beads could always be found in the same basket along with the Leggs pantyhose plastic container. Pop Shoppe pop, KFC, and soft ice cream cones were a must each summer. It was always a fun-filled week spent there with my cousins.

I had kept in touch with my dad's family through the years by visiting them at weddings and various get-togethers. I had always felt close to my aunts, especially my Aunt Myrna. Remember, she was the one who came and helped with us when we were little girls back when my dad was still alive. Since we were pretty close, it was fairly easy for me to pick up the phone and give her a call to see if she had any information about my half-sibling. "Hi, Aunt Myrna. It's Wendy calling. How are you doing?" I asked. In my mind, I was going over how I was going to ask her what I wanted to know.

"Oh fine. And yourself?" she replied.

"I'm doing good."

"How are Jim and Darian?" She was probably wondering why I was calling.

"They are both doing well, Aunt Myrna. What about your family? How's everyone doing?" I wanted to make small talk and gradually ease into my question.

"Fine, fine. They're all doing fine." I'm sure she told me what everyone was up to but I can't remember the details.

"Well, the reason I'm calling, Aunt Myrna, is I was

wondering if you remember anything about my dad having a child with a woman named Nancy?"

"Yes, yes I do. What do you want to know?" she asked.

At this point, I wasn't sure how much she would be willing to tell me and I was feeling a bit nervous about asking something that could be quite personal and emotional. I shouldn't have worried. She was like a fountain of information flowing over after having been dammed up for twenty-six years.

My dad's sister was more than happy to offer what she knew about the child and the history behind the girl and my dad. She shared that I had a half-brother! And she had a picture of him and his mom Nancy from one of her visits to the Children's Aid Society. He had been given up for adoption after all. She didn't have a name but remembered the birth month was either June or July. Aunt Myrna told me his mom's maiden name, Nancy Gunness, along with other pertinent information. She was somehow related to my Uncle Eddie, who was married to my dad's sister Auntie Fay. Nancy was now married with two children and living in the same town as my aunt. She even gave me her phone number. That conversation hadn't been so hard after all. The difficult part would be calling Nancy after all these years and seeing if she would help me find my half-brother.

Aunt Myrna did tearfully confide that she regretted not adopting the baby herself. She and her husband had discussed it at the time but since they already had two small children, they both felt they had enough on their plate.

When I hung up I was overwhelmed with excitement over having a half-brother. The possibility of having a brother instead of a sister had in part compelled me to look for this person in the first place. Growing up in a house without a male presence was challenging. We all took turns cutting the grass, putting out the garbage, fixing bike chains, shovelling snow, and doing other chores that, at least in the 1960s and 1970s, were usually done by boys or the man of the house. I missed being told I was "Daddy's little girl" or hearing "You look so beautiful today, honey" from a man. There was nothing masculine about our home, only sugar and spice.

Anyways, I now had the mother's full name, current address, and phone number. Maybe I'd have another male in my life soon. But it had been twenty-six long years since this woman had given up her firstborn son for adoption and lost her boyfriend so tragically all within a month. What were the chances the next call would go as well as my call to Aunt Myrna? Full cooperation would be optimal, but I needed to be prepared for denials or being hung up on. "Leave well enough alone" and "None of your business" were likely responses to my questioning. She's married with two grown children now, and I thought about how that might make a difference. Her husband and children may not know about her secret. Well, there was only one way to find out. Call her.

CHAPTER SIXTEEN

THE CALL

1993

Before I called Nancy, I wanted more reassurance that this was even a good idea. My mom had grudgingly consented and Aunt Myrna was behind me. Of course Jim was fully on board. So who else could I turn to for encouragement? My two sisters, of course! As you learned in Part One, we navigated many obstacles together while growing up creating a bond between us like no other.

Let me remind you about my two sisters. Wanda, we call her "Blondie" because of her hair, was the oldest and tended to be bossy, but she wanted what was best for us. She always knew how to make me feel truly loved. Linda, we call her "Pudge" because of her little nose and round face, was the baby of the family. She always went along with whatever Wanda and I threw at her. She is so easy going and nothing seems to bother her. I count on her to lift my spirits. We were all married by this point and had at least one child. Linda was married to steadfast and secure Joe and had a son named Devin. Wanda's first marriage resulted in two beautiful boys, Jeremy and Derek, but it had ended in divorce. She had remarried the previous year to John—he loved and adored her. He was so different from her first husband. This guy was a keeper. Look at that! We each married a "J" guy ... John, Jim, and Joe. I promise it wasn't planned, but nothing beats a fun coincidence.

It was time to call my sisters and let them know I had found out our half-sibling was actually our half-brother. Was it time to inject some male perspective into our family? Would they think it was a good idea for me to reach out to Nancy? They couldn't believe we had a brother. A baby brother at that. Now mind you, he would be twenty-six years old at this point, but still, a younger brother. Both of my sisters said they were one hundred percent behind me if finding him was something I wanted to do.

Their emotional support was all I needed to proceed. I just had to get up the guts for the next move. I had to put aside all my shyness, insecurities, overanalyzing and just go for it. Somehow I had to muster up the courage and just focus on the end goal—finding him. A few days later I finally called Nancy. Some of the details are a little fuzzy, but I vividly remember my shaking hands, sweaty palms, and pounding heart.

Thoughts were swirling in my mind. What if she hung up on me? How would I cope with rejection? To increase the chances she'd talk to me, I decided to focus on my search for my half-brother. I'd try to leave my dad out of it. I could have accused her of stealing my father away from me and my family, but in all honesty he was a grown man when he made that decision. Unfortunately for him, the choice led to his death.

When Nancy answered the phone and I introduced myself she moved to a private room. I took this as a good sign. Great relief flooded over me when she was receptive to working with me in my search. There was never a word of animosity between us, only civil exchanges between two adult women. I explained how I didn't want him to feel alone in this world when he had three half-sisters. My life had been great with my sisters and I knew we had lots of friendship, and even possibly love, to share with him one day.

Nancy was aware of Alaric, my stillborn son. She admitted to visiting my father's grave where both of them were buried together. It shocked me she still visited my father's grave after all the time that had passed. She must have truly loved him. How surprised she must have been on the day she discovered the small flat grave marker for my son. From then on, there would be a physical stone to mark where they both rested. Before Alaric had been laid to rest there was no indication as to where the actual gravesite was. A headstone had never been placed there for my father, by either his parents or my mother.

Nancy expressed her deepest sympathy for my loss and I was genuinely touched. I felt a connection with this woman since we had both lost children, albeit in very different ways. Her marriage now had blessed her with two more sons. I asked her if either of them knew about the baby. She explained her husband did but not her boys. I had written a list of questions to ask her during our call. Here's what I learned.

Nancy Aileen Gunness ... her full maiden name.

Dwayne Michael Gunness ... his full name at birth.

Yes ... my dad was definitely the father.

Yes ... my dad was named as the father at the time of adoption, but Dwayne maintained her surname as she and Leonard hadn't been married.

Yes ... he was given up for adoption after my father died but she didn't remember the date.

Yes ... it was through the London Children's Aid Society (C.A.S.) and not a private agency.

No ... .she had not tried to contact him or register anywhere for contact and information.

St. Joseph's Hospital London ... place of birth.

June 1967 ... date of birth, but she couldn't remember the day.

Eight months old ... when he was adopted. To her knowledge, he was put into a foster home first and then moved to his forever home after that.

Nancy also shared with me the events of that fateful night twenty-six years ago, and the impact it had on her. She recalled being sedated as a result of witnessing the horrific scene and running screaming down the street completely in a state of shock.

I asked her if she wanted to meet Dwayne when I found him. She declined, expressing how that period of her life had been extremely traumatic, and she didn't want to dredge up all those horrific memories. But she also said that not a day went by that she didn't think of my dad and her baby Dwayne and what could have been. I respected her decision, but it was difficult for me to understand after I had gone through so much to have my son, Darian. Not knowing him would drive me crazy. Could she possibly have some guilt and regret about her choices? Could seeing Dwayne really bring back her trauma? Only Nancy knew the answers.

After about an hour, I thanked her for the immense help and hung up. Wow! I had a name, part of Dwayne's birth date, his birth parents' full names, and where he was put up for adoption. I bet I was just a few phone calls away from finding him.

Does a few mean two, three, or could it turn into twenty-three?

CHAPTER SEVENTEEN

ZERO PERCENT

March 1994

"Wendy, you have a zero percent chance of getting pregnant again," my doctor stated. The recent results of my hysterosalpingogram were in, and after a year of Jim and I trying to conceive again the outcome was grim. We had both been tested every which way possible and finally had the reason why nothing was happening. During this last procedure, they used an X-ray and dye to examine my uterus and fallopian tubes and discovered both of my tubes were blocked. Nothing could pass through to my uterus, which of course meant no more babies. I couldn't believe what I was hearing. How could this happen to us? What did I do to cause this? Whenever I get devastating news, I have no initial emotional reaction.

I take a long time to process it, often overanalyzing it, and then really reacting later when I'm alone.

At this time, I believed in God but wasn't practicing my faith. I had been married in a church but that's where it stopped. Having the upbringing I did, though, and going to church regularly, had taught me to pray daily. Later that night, before bed, I prayerfully cried, "Dear Lord. Why are all these bad things happening to me? What did I ever do to deserve this? There must be a reason why all this is happening to me, but right now I don't understand." I tried not to become angry with God, but it was becoming more and more difficult. Every horrifying tragedy had me questioning if there truly was a God. If there was, why would he allow all this to happen?

It was easy to let self-pity and blame rule my life. When I did, that old gray, sad, and hopeless feeling would try to creep back in. Thinking about Dwayne, though, would re-centre me and pull me to the present. My life was blessed with my sisters, but what about Dwayne? How was he feeling? He would be twenty-seven years old. An adult. Was he married with children of his own? I needed to find out.

CHAPTER EIGHTEEN

JUST CALL ME SHERLOCK

March-September 1994

I was excited to start my search, and thanks to my stellar detective skills I already had the first clue. During our phone call, Nancy had mentioned she had placed Dwayne in the care of the C.A.S..

Before contacting the organization, though, I had discovered that a birth relative of an adoptee can register with the Adoption Disclosure Register (Ontario). If the adoptee has registered also, the two applications are matched up and arrangements are made for a meeting. This was one way of finding Dwayne if he was looking for his birth family. I completed the application and hoped for a speedy response.

They mailed me confirmation of my registration

along with an information sheet of other avenues I could explore. Parent Finders was one of the options … they were a self-help group formed by adoptees and adoptive and birth parents. The group was run by volunteers who provided support for those searching for a family member.

In the meantime, I continued my detective work. As I dialled the number for the C.A.S., I was quite nervous and wondered if they would share information with me. The person I first spoke with would not reveal anything. I was asked to call back later in the week. I waited a few days and then finally Friday came and I tried again. I was delighted to discover Dwayne had been adopted through the London agency. This would make my search so much easier. I asked what my next step should be and the worker gave me the name of someone in their agency to contact. I was transferred to her but my call went straight to voicemail, so I would have to call back later.

After several tries, I finally got a hold of my contact person on March 17, 1994. She said I could be put on a waiting list to receive "non-identifying information." This means the information would contain nothing specific to identify the child; it would only be basic facts about his birth, developmental health history, placement history, and adoptive parents. I was shocked to learn about the wait time. She explained, "It could take from two to two-and-a-half years to compile the information. There are many people in line ahead of you. If and when you do receive the file, it'll go to Sarnia Children's Aid Society because we don't mail information. Do you want to proceed?" That seemed like a long time to wait, but I had no other option. I agreed to be put on the list.

While I waited for information on Dwayne, I slowly realized that Darian was growing into a little man who needed me less and less. We had Jim's income and it was enough to get by, but we agreed it would be nice to have some extra money and to save for Darian's education. Maybe it was time for me to work towards reentering the workforce.

I was excited when I noticed an ad in the local paper. It was for a government-funded program that paid for individuals to take classes and it covered childcare costs as well. After completing The In-Home Daycare Providers Training Program, I could eventually run my own home daycare and have all the benefits of working without having to leave Darian in the care of others. I immediately enrolled after I secured daycare in Inwood for Darian. The course included all aspects of having a daycare in your home, including co-op placements and the financial side of owning a home business. This was a very unique and exciting opportunity for me. I loved the course, learned so much, and was ready to open my home daycare shortly after graduation.

I started my home daycare with only one child at first, and Ben came in the mornings, every other day. Ben's mom did the mail run, which involved delivering mail to rural customers with mailboxes at the roadside. The boy was a friend of Darian's, so it was an excellent arrangement as they had each other to play with. The days I didn't look after Ben, both he and Darian attended junior kindergarten when school started in September, leaving me at home with plenty of time on my hands.

I used the days alone at home to continue my search for Dwayne. I started with the local county building and connected with a woman in the History Department there. She suggested I call Sarnia and London Public Libraries and ask for the Reference Department. If I had a full name and city, the Reference Department could search in the coordinating city directory for information on that person. I learned telephone directories were current at the library but they also retained archived copies and city directories as well. The information in these directories would be more thorough than just your typical telephone book, she explained. The Genealogical Society of Middlesex was also included on her list and she provided me with the telephone number.

Any of these suggestions could have helped me if I found more information like the adoptive parents' or child's new name. Having the adoptive parents' names would be beneficial, but since I didn't have that information I started with Dwayne's given name at birth even though the chances of it being changed to protect the child's identity were very high. Once you were adopted, you became a member of your new family and that meant taking on their surname.

Since London was the city where Dwayne was adopted by his new family, it made sense to check out the telephone book for that city or to call directory assistance to see if there was a current listing. Calling seemed the quickest and easiest so that was my first go-to. I was counting on Dwayne not moving from his hometown as an adult—the odds might be in my favour since London was a fairly large city with lots of employment opportunities. Much to my disappointment, though, when I called 411 I found out there was no listing for Dwayne in London or any of the surrounding areas. I broadened the range and kept calling the operator back, but this did not provide any results.

I had previously worked at a small telephone office in Inwood for a few years, helping out with billing and vacation relief. I knew they must have accumulated a multitude of phone books since they were reluctant to throw them out. After explaining the reason for my enquiry, they were more than happy to give me free reign over all the phone books they had. And it just so happened there were quite a few London phone books in their collection. I searched for Dwayne Michael Gunness every which way I could and even broadened my investigation to the surrounding small towns listed in the London phone book. With my stubbornness and determination,

I checked through pretty much every phone book they had. But nothing.

The next time Darian was at school I called the Genealogical Society. I was stoked to get things moving and was convinced I would finally get some leads. The woman who answered there told me I could request a birth certificate for twenty-two dollars. I wrote down the official address, but I must have hit a dead end. I don't recall filing any paperwork with the Office of the Registrar General. I vaguely remember them telling me I needed to provide proof of the birth when I put in the paperwork, and I knew I didn't have that.

No sense wasting the day, so I placed another call to the C.A.S. My last call was six months earlier and maybe they would have an update. Last time, my contact person had encouraged me to check in from time to time and seemed willing to cooperate. When I spoke to her this time she reminded me again of the two-and-a-half year wait time, and since it had only been six months since my request for the information, it would still likely be another two years until I got an answer. She must have heard the disappointment in my voice and my determination to find Dwayne because she made a helpful suggestion. She let me know some adoptive families put an announcement in the newspaper about the adoption and keywords used were often "chosen son" or "chosen daughter." "Okay, now we're getting somewhere," I thought. Another clue for the detective.

By this point I knew libraries kept archives of telephone and city directories, but I wondered if they did the same for newspapers. Once again I headed to the phone and called Sarnia Public Library.

Before I forget to mention this, you should realize the internet was not part of everyday life in 1994. All my research was done the old-fashioned way, using directory assistance or the phone book for phone numbers and accessing the library for everything else. It wasn't until the late 1990s when home computers and the internet were widely available and affordable. No doubt the internet would have made my search easier, but also it would have made it a less exciting adventure.

A phone call to Sarnia Public Library revealed newspapers could indeed be accessed through microfiche. Microfiche is similar to a picture film and you insert it into a machine to enlarge the image. The only problem now was finding time to physically go to the Sarnia library to access their files. Sarnia was at least half an hour from Inwood, which meant an hour round trip. Would it be worth giving up my time and gas money for something that may result in another dead end?

CHAPTER NINETEEN

MORE SLEUTHING

September-October 1994

By the fall of 1994 I had become braver in my attempt to find Dwayne. Aunt Myrna had given me the name of a woman who Nancy had gone to live with after my father's death. She might be able to give me valuable information. I just needed to muster up the courage to cold-call Mrs. Rawlinson. It had been twenty-seven years. Would she remember anything?

"Hello, Mrs. Rawlinson?"

"Yes. This is she. And you are?" a woman's voice on the other end cautiously inquired.

"You don't know me, but I'm Wendy Scott. I'm searching for my half brother, who was born in 1967, and I was told that his mother, Nancy Gunness, may have stayed with you briefly just after his birth. Would you be willing to answer a few questions?" I was so nervous, but any clue leading to Dwayne was worth it. I had to learn how to respond if someone hung up, yelled, or said, "It's none of your business!"

"Hi, Wendy. Yes, most certainly I remember Nancy and will help you with any information you need." Mrs. Rawlinson was kind and courteous even when she didn't have to answer any questions. I must have sounded sincere enough for her to want to help. "Do you remember when exactly Nancy came to stay with you?"

"She came one week after my twins were born on July 31, 1967. I needed lots of help with them in the beginning as there was so much work to do. Having two babies was exhausting and Nancy gave me the relief I needed for about three weeks," she shared.

Since she was responding well to my questions and seemed open and honest, I proceeded with my next, and most important, question, "My next question may sound a little odd, but could you please tell me if she had a baby with her?"

She responded, "No. There was no baby with her. Is there anything else you would like to know?"

Knowing where Nancy went next could be somewhat helpful. I asked, "After leaving your house, do you know where Nancy went?"

"No, I'm sorry, dear. I lost touch with her after that," she answered.

"Thank you for your time, Mrs. Rawlinson. You've

been most helpful. I can't think of anything else right now to ask, but could I call you if I need any more information?"

Mrs. Rawlinson said I could call her anytime if I had more questions. I couldn't believe her willingness to help a stranger and inwardly hoped all people would be so eager to aid in my search.

So now I had some dates to work with. Dwayne was probably given up for adoption sometime between July 22, 1967 and August 7, 1967. Nancy had said it was sometime after my father's death, which was July 22, but she was unsure of the exact date. Since Mrs. Rawlinson's twins were born July 31, 1967, and Nancy came one week later, it would mean it was August 7, 1967 when she went to help with the twins. When Nancy came to stay with her, she had no baby with her. These dates were crucial for what I was about to embark on next.

I was somewhat apprehensive when I thought about travelling to Sarnia and learning how to use their microfiche system. I wanted to learn new technology as much as I wanted to walk across a bed of hot coals. Not pleasant but necessary to move forward. And the Sarnia trips would take so much time. It would be an hour of my day just in driving, plus time to examine and explore each newspaper ad containing adoption notices. A part of me said, "Yes. You can do this." Another part of me said, "What for?

You're not going to find him anyways. It's like finding a needle in a haystack."

My stubbornness and perseverance won the battle.

Driving to Sarnia, I crossed my fingers with the hope that the adoptive parents resided in London in 1968. People move away, get divorced. You know, life happens. I may be able to track them down if they left London, but I needed a starting point. This adoption happened twenty-seven years ago, so I figured I'd be counting on clues in old newspapers.

The librarian in Sarnia helped me immensely. She set up the microfiche reader with the sheets of film I needed, demonstrating how to use it. Since I knew the exact date of my father's death, I began with *The London Free Press* articles around that date. My mom had once shown me a newspaper clipping of the front page of an article that covered the shooting, so I knew one existed.

It was fairly easy to find as I scanned the magnified images. There on the front page of July 22, 1967 was a photo of my handsome dad and the story of his death. Looking at the image, I thought about how surreal my father's death had always seemed to me as a child. Like I said in an earlier chapter, it was a story told to us about our dad but it never seemed real. Now it did. It was right before my very eyes in black and white. I read the story over and over again, discovering a new bit of information each time. The last read through I convinced myself to put it down and move on to the next phase. This part was going to be much more difficult as I didn't know exactly what I was looking for.

I knew Dwayne had been given up around July 1967, and based on previous research, I had learned it took at least six months for an adoption to be completed. This would bring the final adoption around January, so to play it safe, I searched for all of 1968. After finding the birth announcements section of *The London Free Press*, I would skim and scan for the words: "adopted," "chosen," and "son." Dwayne's birth date was irrelevant at this point because the announcements did not have dates or birth weights. They were merely a formality to present, or welcome, the new adopted son or daughter into the family.

So, this became my routine whenever Darian was at school or Jim was free to watch him. I would drive to Sarnia Public Library, continue where I left off from the previous visit, and write down word for word (no cellphone cameras back then) the information I found. Each time meant having to find the right films, so I became a pro at this microfiche stuff. After loading the machine, I painstakingly scrutinized every birth announcement in *The London Free Press* for that year. I cannot begin to guess how many visits it took to complete my task, but I can tell you I accumulated thirty-one names throughout my many visits. It was a lot of work, but the next part was even more challenging.

My search in *The London Free Press* birth announcements was done under the assumption the adoptive family resided in London in 1968 and remained there. This adoption had happened so many years ago. Was it even possible for Dwayne or his adoptive parents to still be living in London in 1994?

I got smart and borrowed the most current London phone books from the telephone office in Inwood. This way I wasn't rushed and could research in my spare time. Once I was through looking in all the phone books and had compiled a list, I started calling 411 to fill in any gaps since I knew the phone books were not totally up to date. The only problem with calling 411 was the cost. Each time you called, they would only give you one listing for fifty cents. I remembered that the lady at the county building had suggested calling the Reference Department at London Public Library and so I gave it a shot.

Good thing I did. They could give me three listings from the city directories along with the address and head of the household's occupation. This was great news for me and must have been the extra information the lady from the county had spoken about. Another clue to store away for future use. I never knew city directories would list occupations. Since London's city directories dated back to 1968, I asked for that listing plus a current one, trying every possible angle I could think of.

Now the order in which the cold calls and research occurred is not necessarily important at this point. And I honestly can't recall my strategy. It would make sense if I called each number after receiving it, and crossed it off my list as I went along. It would be a lot of calls to make at one time, even for someone as determined as me. I still have my lists of adoptive parents from back in 1994. After analyzing it one day, I realized that eight out of the thirty-one parents still resided in London then. The lists contain the addresses, phone numbers, and special notes regarding my contact with them.

My spiel for each call would start with a brief introduction of who I was. I'd explain they didn't know me but that I was calling to find my half brother who was adopted in 1968. Just like Mrs. Rawlinson, people were more than willing to help me. No one was rude, no one hung up, and no one told me to mind my own business. Really, it's astonishing it went so smoothly. My confidence grew and I gained a new perspective. Sometimes I second-guessed myself and wondered if I was doing the right thing. I would then remind myself of how helpful people were being. It was natural to want to find adoptees. Soon, though, disappointment from hearing, "No. I'm sorry but you have the wrong person. My son was born on ... " began to wear me down. The rejections became increasingly harder as the list grew shorter.

On top of that, Jim and I were still struggling with trying to grow our family. During a visit with our family doctor, we discussed options. They were in vitro fertilization, adoption, and a visit to a fertility specialist. I was scared when they mentioned in vitro as I was worried it was risky plus it didn't seem natural. The other two options seemed viable though. Jim admitted he didn't feel adoption was right for him and he felt in vitro could be costly. He suggested we see the fertility specialist and go from there. We called our family doctor back and booked an appointment with the specialist. The earliest appointment available was for the summer of the following year, 1995. Although it was only eight months away it seemed like a lifetime.

CHAPTER TWENTY

LEAVING A LETTER

October 1994

It was time again to call the C.A.S. for an update. I made it a priority to check in every few months just in case there was a break in my case. You never know, Dwayne could have reached out and contacted them. I wanted to remain current and consistent, and it seemed like every time I called new clues were revealed. This time was no different.

"Hi. It's Wendy Scott calling again about Dwayne Gunness. Are there any updates to his file?" I asked.

"Sorry, Mrs. Scott. I have no new information to give you," the contact person responded.

"Has Dwayne ever contacted your agency before?" I asked.

"We would have checked this when you registered for

non-identifying information. You can leave a letter in his file, explaining yourself and any information you feel he may want to know."

This was news to me. "Like what kind of information are you talking about?" I questioned.

"Medical history about your family, personal history about yourself, siblings, or anything he may want to know, but nothing identifiable," she shared.

"Okay. I want to do that. How does it work?" I asked.

"Just send in the information along with a letter waiving confidentiality. If Dwayne were to come into our office looking for information, we would show the letter to him," she replied.

"I'm going to get right on this, so expect it in the mail within the next week. Thank you so much for all your help." I ended the call feeling elated by this new knowledge.

I have included a copy of my letter on the next page. Although there is no identifiable information, I worded the letter in such a way that Dwayne could hopefully figure out how to find me. The sentence about our biological father where it says "He was killed shortly after your birth" was a big clue. I thought if Dwayne wanted to, he could solve the mystery by digging around in old newspapers and archives like I had been doing and eventually find me. It was worth a shot.

Many a time I speculated if he wanted to know who his birth parents were. All he had to do was ask me. I was hoping he grew up in a home where his adoptive parents had been open about his adoption and had encouraged him to find his birth family if he ever felt the need to search them out.

October 19, 1994

DWAYNE MICHAEL GUNNESS

I have left this information in the event you should contact The hondon Children's Aid Society and request any family or medical background.

I am your half'sister since we both had the same biological father. He was killed shortly after your birth and one day before my fourth birthday. I am married, live in a very small town, and have one child at present My son, an only child, has made me realize what you may be feeling unless you were raised with other siblings.

You have two more half sisters and two more half brothers that I know of.

Our grandfather is a diabetic but no other family member has inherited this disease that I am aware of.

I just wanted to let you know you are being thought of and if things work out we will meet some day.

After I left this letter at the C.A.S., I immediately felt hopeful I'd find Dwayne. I believed he would walk into their agency any day and we would find each other. My prayers would be answered and finally we would both have closure. Of course it was all wishful thinking, but I had nothing to lose.

At this point I remembered when I registered with the Adoption Disclosure Registry they had mentioned an organization called Parent Finders. I called 411 to see if there was a group in London. Bingo! After jotting down the phone number, I promptly hung up and dialled Parent Finders. In my head, I was rehearsing what I wanted to say, but unfortunately my call was picked up by an answering machine. I was too anxious and unsure to leave a message. So I hung up and wrote down exactly what I wanted to say. The next time I dialled and the recording came on, I read out the words I had prepared. It's amazing the confidence a little pre-planning can give you.

Two days later, a Parent Finders volunteer returned my call. After the initial pleasantries, he answered the question I'd left on the answering machine.

"Mrs. Scott, you asked if Dwayne has ever registered with us, but sadly I can't find any record of it," he reported.

"I was so wishing he had. Since he was adopted in London, it would make sense for him to contact London Parent Finders. He must not be looking for his birth family yet."

My disappointment must have been palpable as he sincerely offered his advice and help.

"Mrs. Scott, looking for a family member can be like a waiting game. It all depends on whether the person wants to be found or is even looking for their birth family. When both members finally meet up it can be a very wonderful thing, but until then I suggest you try to be patient. In the meantime, we have a computer registry that provides a province-wide search. The cost is twenty-five dollars."

After I thanked him, he added, "I will contact A.I.E. (Adoption Information Exchange) in Sarnia to see if our registry is connected with theirs. That way you can keep in touch with Sarnia since that's closer for you. Why don't you think about joining their group?"

"Okay, I'll think about it and about joining the computer registry. I believe he's in London, so I'm just not sure it would be beneficial to search elsewhere." I honestly felt this way and stood firm in my belief that I'd find Dwayne in London. It was too overwhelming to think he could be anywhere else. The world is a big place. Just having London to focus on was easy peasy.

CHAPTER TWENTY-ONE

HOPE GROWS

July-October 1995

By now my home daycare had two more permanent children and the odd part-timers. My days were filled with songs, meals, painting, playdough, arts and crafts, outdoor play, circle time, nap time, and planning for the following week. I had a theme-based daycare where every week we had a different topic to learn about and enjoy. I thoroughly loved working with children and watching them explore and discover themselves through play and friendships. Having the daycare allowed Darian, an only child, the opportunity to make new friends and learn social skills with children his age. He attended school every other day still, but I didn't have any more free time on those days as I had my full time daycare children then.

Having a business in your own home can be challenging,

especially when your spouse works shift work. There were many days where I tried to have the children play outside as much as possible so Jim could get the rest he needed. Of course, the children loved this. We made chalk train tracks and roads on the paved laneway for their ride-on toys, played in the sandbox with dinky cars and trucks, went for walks and had picnics at the park, painted the garage with brushes dipped in water, blew bubbles ... really, we did just about anything the parent magazines and educational resources suggested were fun things to do.

Being the only adult among all those little ones was also challenging at times. Sometimes I wished we lived in a bigger town so we could join other playgroups or home daycares. I craved adult conversation and looked forward to the end of the day when the parents picked their children up so we could share stories about our day. Feedback from parents was what kept me motivated as a home daycare provider. Each one would share how much they appreciated my creativity and the care their children received in my home.

Summer finally came which meant no more school, so all my daycare kids and Darian were with me every weekday. It also was time for something else. The day had finally come to visit the fertility specialist in London. I booked the day off so parents had to find alternative care for their children. Darian went to a friend's house, leaving Jim and me able to direct our full attention to the specialist and our options.

Our family physician had highly recommended this specialist so I felt confident he could help us. Added to that was the fact he was located in London. London is home to Western University, which produces top-notch medical research and doctors. So going into the hospital, I prayed for support, guidance, and a way past our zero percent chance of conceiving.

The specialist gave us the answers we wanted to hear. He was willing to do exploratory surgery and find out if there was a way to clear my blocked fallopian tubes. There would only be a few small incisions and I would be under general anesthesia. He explained my tubes could be blocked with scar tissue from the ectopic pregnancy or maybe endometriosis was this issue. Endometriosis occurs when tissue that lines the uterus attaches and grows outside the uterus, such as on the ovaries or the fallopian tubes. We discussed the risks of surgery, in vitro fertilization, and my blocked tubes.

All of us agreed having the surgery was the best option. The specialist felt certain it was worth the risks and he had a high success rate with this particular surgery. We went ahead and booked the next available date which was in October. That would give me plenty of time to both mentally prepare myself and to make childcare arrangements for Darian and my daycare kids.

Having so much time to think about the actual surgery and what the procedure beforehand would entail caused me a lot of anxiety. When I had the ectopic pregnancy, there wasn't any choice in the matter and no length of time to worry and stress about the possible outcomes. It was either have the surgery and live, or wait until the tube exploded and possibly die. That time it was a no brainer. This time, I had four months to play over all the scenarios in my head until the proverbial cows came home. I tried putting all my time and effort into my home daycare to distract myself.

I also came across an article on successful surgery outcomes and how to mentally prepare beforehand to decrease your recovery time. It made sense to me that if you entered into surgery with good thoughts, you would come out more relaxed and your surgery would go smoother. I had heard of people waking up during their surgery and thrashing about so much that the procedure had to be aborted. They all had felt stressed before their surgery and had not been confident in their surgeon's ability to perform well. I was not going to allow that to happen, so I mentally prepared myself in advance to remain calm and practice positive thinking.

On October 4, 1995 a message was left on my answering machine from the C.A.S. My contact person asked if I could return her call, but I was focused on my surgery which was scheduled for the following day. I tried to remain calm by not thinking about her reasons for calling me. I knew my search for Dwayne would have to be put on hold until after my surgery.

On October 5, 1995 I went into the surgery with

a zero percent chance of ever getting pregnant again. I came out of the surgery with a fifty percent chance of conceiving. The specialist explained to Jim and me how he had made a few small incisions in my abdomen and pelvic area to enable him to perform a laparoscopic procedure. Upon exploration, he diagnosed the problem and proceeded using laser laparoscopy, removing tissue from my right fallopian tube. Since my tubal pregnancy had occurred in the left tube, the chance of it happening again in the same tube was greatly increased. But now that I had one functioning tube, from my perspective I was fifty percent closer to growing my family.

A few days later, I was thinking about how things were looking up for our little family. Darian was in senior kindergarten and playing hockey, Jim had plenty of work and was thrilled to be a hockey parent, and I was enjoying my home daycare. We decided to wait a month or so for me to have a regular period and then try again for another baby. Everything seemed to be falling into place.

Then I remembered the message on my answering machine from my contact person at the C.A.S. While I dialled the number, plenty of scenarios played through my mind. Maybe Dwayne had contacted their agency and was asking to meet me after reading the letter I left in his file. He could have just contacted the agency and now they were notifying me. I thought it definitely couldn't be the non-identifying information report as I had only been put on the list a year and a half ago and I had been told it could take two or two and a half years to hear anything.

I waited patiently as the operator connected me. But my mind was a flurry of excitement and I'm sure my words were jumbled as I said, "Hi. It's Wendy Scott returning your call from October 4."

"Yes, Mrs. Scott. I had called to give you an update on your file but needed to tell you in person, not on your answering machine," she said with a hint of elation.

"Okay. What's the update?" I was hoping this was going to be the break I needed, but at the same time I didn't want to get my hopes up.

"Your non-identifying information report has been completed. You should receive it within the month. I'm mailing it directly to you. Please let me know when you receive it." Her voice revealed the delight she felt sharing this wonderful news.

I was ecstatic and thanked her profusely. This information could be crucial in finding Dwayne. My thoughts immediately went to its contents and what non-identifying information would be revealed for me to use in my search. All that month, I wondered how this next clue would help solve the puzzle.

CHAPTER TWENTY-TWO

GOOD NEWS AND BIGGER CHALLENGES

October 30, 1995

Hockey season can be a very busy time for young families. The children come home from school tired and hungry, grab a quick bite to eat, and then head out to the rink. This particular night, Darian had hockey practice and was trying to eat the light supper I had prepared but he was tired from a full day at school and just wasn't coping well. He didn't want to go, but after some coaxing he ate, got dressed, and headed to the arena with his dad. This left me alone with my report.

Did I forget to mention the report from the C.A.S. had finally arrived in the mail? I had retrieved our mail earlier that morning when I took the daycare kids for our daily walk and there it was. I couldn't wait to open it when I got home. I quickly scanned it when I got the chance but didn't have enough time to analyze it the way I had wanted to. Now, I had lots of time to carefully read it over without being disturbed.

The three-page report contained the non-identifying information about Dwayne. Its cover letter stated that I had requested the information in March 1994. Since the agency had predicted a possible wait time of two and a half years, I was happy to have only waited nineteen months. The agency encouraged me to keep my current address updated with the Adoption Registry in Toronto (an adoption disclosure registry I had also registered with in 1994). The cover letter closed with a phone number should I have any questions about the information contained in the report.

I was overjoyed after reading how Dwayne was portrayed in the letter. He was described as being an attractive, healthy, and happy baby boy. He had been developing and progressing well during each check in. This eased my mind, as knowing the young age of his birth mother, I had a few concerns as to whether she had taken care of herself properly during the pregnancy.

The most useful fact I read was Dwayne's birthdate, June 15, 1967, since Nancy had trouble remembering the exact date. This was an important piece of the puzzle I could use in my search.

The next thing that caught my attention was the date Dwayne was placed in the temporary care of the C.A.S.:

July 15, 1967. This meant Dwayne could not possibly have been with Nancy the night of the shooting on July 22 ... unless his foster home had been with the Roby family. The report stated he went directly to a foster home after being put in temporary care. *The London Free Press* reported only three Roby children were present during the shooting. There was no mention of a baby. We will discuss this theory more in a later chapter, so stay tuned.

From the report I also learned the final adoption order was signed in 1968. This information was very vague but coincided with my belief that the adoption process took at least six months. January of 1968 was where I had begun my search for Dwayne in the newspaper birth announcements but had found no leads.

When the letter revealed the occupations of the adoptive parents, I was once again put into detective mode remembering how telephone directories listed these. Along with their occupations, the report listed physical descriptions and personalities. I envisaged how this new information could help me find my brother. I still did not have any real names, only Dwayne's name at birth.

Knowing that his adoptive parents were open to discussions about adoption, I felt Dwayne might already know his history. This could make things easier for me, especially if I found him. He would not be in shock, possibly accept me as his half-sister, and want to join his extended family. It was also highly possible that if he knew about his adoption, one day he would feel compelled to find his birth parents or family. The worst-case scenario was hard to even imagine. What if he did not want to be found? This was unthinkable, so I bulldozed this idea right back to where it came from—that deep dark pit of negative thoughts. From now on, I promised myself to only concentrate on positive outcomes.

Those first few weeks after I received the report on Dwayne, I studied it repeatedly. I analyzed it trying to get some hints and clues as to who these people were. Dwayne's adoptive dad being a beverage company salesman really didn't help me. But his adoptive mom being a nurse? That just might be useful. I called St. Joseph's Hospital in London and asked if they kept employee records as far back as 1967. Since the letter had stated the mother was a nurse before she adopted the baby, I considered the possibility of her working at a hospital up until that time. The employee said they did not keep records that long. Even if they had, I wondered if it would be confidential information anyway. I felt anything was worth a try. Nothing ventured, nothing gained.

A conversation with someone whose name I can't recall led me to think about graduation nursing books. There must be some type of book with every person who graduated from nursing school. I called Parent Finders in London to ask for their assistance but came up empty. They knew of no such book.

As my ideas and leads started to dwindle, so too did my hopes of finding Dwayne. The report had seemed so promising. It was a tough blow with nothing significant coming from it. And to top things off I was feeling overly emotional. I wonder what was causing that? I couldn't possibly be pregnant! Jim and I hadn't been trying for that long since my surgery. "Let's be realistic and not get too excited," I thought to myself. But no matter what I did, the food didn't taste great and my stomach felt upset in the morning. Jim was astonished when I mentioned we might be pregnant so soon. Nevertheless, he picked up a pregnancy test on the way home from work the next day and we waited to see the results. Positive. The test was positive! I wanted to scream, "Hallelujah! Our prayers have been answered!" But I wanted to get confirmation before fully buying into my excitement. I remained calm and told Jim I needed more proof so we booked an appointment with my Ob/Gyn for the next day.

I looked forward to seeing my Ob/Gyn. We had become quite close given our frequent visits over the years, developing a good rapport and even sharing a love for knitting. And he had been there during two crucial life-saving moments in my life. I looked up to this man and trusted him completely. When I got to his office, he said, "Mrs. Scott. I know your history and everything you've been through. If you are pregnant, please understand I'll do my best to ensure you receive the best of care. We'll monitor you the whole way through. And we'll arrange for you to have all your ultrasounds at a different hospital where you haven't had a bad experience."

After hearing this, I felt much more relaxed and relieved. Finally, somebody understood what I had gone through and nothing was going to go unnoticed.

Jim and I were thrilled when the tests confirmed I was pregnant. My Ob/Gyn ordered ultrasounds as often as he was allowed. At my appointments, he would read each ultrasound result with me and affirm there really was a baby in my uterus and it was doing fine. He was known for guessing the sex of your baby, and had guessed right with Darian, but unbeknownst to me he always guessed the baby was going to be a boy so he had a fifty-fifty chance of being right. What a guy!

Along with all of the miracle baby celebrations, though, came complications. First, it was my blood sugar levels and then my platelet count. There had been some speculation I had gestational diabetes while pregnant with Darian, but no conclusive results were found. This time there was definitive proof I had gestational diabetes, plus my platelet count dropped more with each passing month. As a result, my pregnancy was considered high-risk, and my medical history only added to the growing concern. That old panic and anxiety was building up in me, and with each new blood test, the fear of losing another baby was heavy on my mind. Sarnia Hospital did not do platelet transfusions, so I was referred to the high-risk clinic in London. At that point, I knew my home daycare would have to be put on hold. I felt my life and the baby's life would be at risk unless I rested, relaxed, and remained calm.

The daycare parents were very disappointed by my news, of course, but they understood my situation completely. With tears in my eyes and hugs for all, I waved goodbye to the parents and their children. There would be no more circle times, crafts, and planning weekly themes for me.

And my search for Dwayne would once again have to go on the back burner. I needed to rest until this baby came. Having two young children would make my life so much busier. Could I juggle my duties as a wife and mother and still find the time to search for Dwayne?

CHAPTER TWENTY-THREE

DELIVERIES

February - August 1996

The first three months of rest went pretty well but then I started getting antsy. With my home daycare on hold and Darian gone every other day for school, I needed some type of diversion. I found myself feeling more relaxed and calm as the pregnancy progressed. Everything was going along smoothly, and I felt absolute confidence in the specialists at the High-Risk Clinic I visited regularly in London. I figured there were no more surprises or complications, so it couldn't hurt to pick up my search for Dwayne.

I started with the Yellow Pages in the London phone book to see if there were any private investigators who could help me. The company I contacted said they would help but at a substantial fee. Since I wasn't working at the time, I scrapped the idea after discussing it with Jim. We just couldn't afford something so extravagant. So I took another route. The investigator had mentioned a company that might be able to help. International Reunion Services (I.R.S.) was a company based out of Hamilton, Ontario. They provided their clients with knowledge of how to search for someone. They would assign a researcher to initiate and complete the search. Their fee was one hundred and fifty dollars for the first three hours and then fifteen dollars per hour for anything above and beyond that time. If I continued my search afterwards on my own, they said I could call there, free of charge, for any additional help. Jim and I agreed the fee seemed reasonable, and after all, the name of the company suggested they were experts at finding and reuniting people—exactly what I needed! This was much less expensive than a private investigator so I went ahead with the registration process. I filled out the application form, which included all the information I knew about Dwayne, and mailed it along with a cheque for the registration fee.

Less than a month later, I received a confirmation letter of my application and fee from I.R.S. Included in this letter was a list of seven questions for me to forward to the C.A.S. Finally, I felt like things were going somewhere. I had people from I.R.S. who could help me take all this non-identifying information and apply it effectively to my search.

The questions I sent to the C.A.S., and their responses, are as follows:

1. Were the adoptive parents born in Canada? **Yes.**

2. Did they live in the city or the countryside? **City.**

3. What is their ethnic background? **English.**

4. Did the adoptive parents have other children? **No.**

5. What is the religion of the adoptive family? **Protestant.**

6. Could they clarify the adoptive father's occupation of beverage company salesman? ie. alcoholic beverages, non-alcoholic beverages, or dairy. **Beverage company salesman is all the information we can provide.**

7. Did the Children's Aid Society of London and Middlesex complete the home inspection for the adoptive family? **We are unable to provide this information as adoptive parents have the right to privacy.**

Some of these questions and answers were interesting, but I didn't know how they would help me find Dwayne. When I sent the answers back to I.R.S. they were not happy with the responses to questions five and seven. They suggested I call the C.A.S. and ask if they would expand on the two answers. Protestant was an umbrella term that encompassed Baptist, United, Presbyterian, and so on. If I could get a more specific answer that might help. Plus the I.R.S. informed me I had a right to know which agency completed the home inspection. If I didn't find out which one, I would have to write to thirty other agencies to find out.

I am by no means a confrontational person. I felt like telling the woman from I.R.S. to call the C.A.S. herself, but I didn't. I knew it was my responsibility to follow through with this so I mustered up the courage to call. Probably by now, the C.A.S. was used to my calls, but it didn't make it any easier. Rocking the boat was not something I wanted to do. So far they had been very helpful.

When I called my contact person at the C.A.S., I explained the reason for needing more information and how the I.R.S. had prompted me to get more specifics. But she would not budge on the Protestant or home inspection answers. She even said it was in their legislation not to reveal who completed the home inspection. After I hung up I hoped I hadn't damaged my relationship with the C.A.S. A few more calls and contact with I.R.S. produced a new lead. One of the names on my list from *The London Free Press* birth announcements came to our attention. I had mailed them the list with my initial registration. The chosen son's name had Dwayne as a middle name and originally I had dismissed it. The city, Wallaceburg, was nowhere near London so I breezed over it thinking it couldn't possibly be him. I reconsidered and called the Wallaceburg Library hoping to get a lead from 1968 or the present day. I found out they did not have city directories dated that far back. They only had back to 1974, and there was no listing for the adoptive parents I was looking for, then or now. Chatham was a larger city close to Wallaceburg, so I tried it too. No luck there either. Quite possibly they could have moved to London at some point so I called the London Public Library, directory assistance, and looked through the current London phone book. I again found nothing. I had exhausted all my resources and considered this lead a dead end.

It was time to take a different approach. I was not giving up. I loved talking to people about my search for Dwayne because it made for interesting conversation, but it also provided additional information for my search. One such conversation led me to a column in *The London Free Press* called "Reader to Reader." It allowed many scenarios to be printed for free, such as my quest to find my half-brother. The column also contained nagging trivia questions, thank-yous, reunions, questions on how to research a book, and pictures people wanted to share—it really was a mixed bag. The only specifics were that you had to write a letter of two hundred words or less. "I can do that," I thought.

April 9, 1996

Reader to Reader
369 York St.
London, Ontario
N6A 4G1

Dear Reader to Reader:

I am searching for my half brother named Dwayne Michael Gunness, born on June 15, 1967 at London's St. Joseph's Hospital.

On July 15, 1967 Dwayne was placed in temporary care of the Children's Aid Society of London. He went directly to a foster home and remained until November 2, 1967 at which time he was moved to a new foster home. He remained at this foster home until he was placed on adoption probation with his adoptive family on January 23, 1968. The final adoption order was signed in 1968 in Ontario.

On November 24, 1967 Dwayne was described as attractive. He was tall, had blonde hair and very blue eyes. His face was long and heart shaped and his complexion was very fair.

The adoptive father was thirty-two years old and worked at a beverage company as a salesman.

The adoptive mother was twenty-eight years old and was a registered nurse planning to leave her job to stay home with Dwayne.

At the time of adoption, Dwayne had no siblings, was of Protestant religion and lived in the city.

Dwayne and I share the same birth father.

I would truly appreciate any information or help in my search.

Yours truly,

Wendy Scott
Box 116
Inwood, Ontario
N0N 1K0
(519)844-2970

My letter was published in the Saturday, May 25, 1996 edition of *The London Free Press*. I carefully chose what I felt was the most important information to put in the column. My goal was to provide as much of the non-identifying information as possible in hopes it would generate a lead. My excitement grew each day after the paper was sent out. I mentally tried to will Dwayne to go and buy that paper so he could find the section and call me immediately.

While I was waiting for some kind of response from my article, I contacted I.R.S. again. My final contact with I.R.S. was in May 1996. My researcher suggested I go to the Provincial Courthouse in London and ask to look at their Action Books for 1967. If asked, I was to say I am looking for an occurrence or happening to my brother during that time. I was directed to look under Crown Wardships for the following possibilities: Middlesex Children's Aid Society, Gunness vs. Middlesex Children's Aid Society, and Children's Aid Society of Middlesex. These were specific suggestions since Dwayne had been made a ward of the C.A.S. of London and Middlesex on October 5, 1967.

Being six months pregnant with our second child and having all the medical concerns to cope with, I decided to just call the London Courthouse instead of making the one hour drive. Having gestational diabetes can cause extreme thirst, frequent urination, and fatigue. I cannot recollect the exact conversation that transpired, only the fact of being no further ahead when it ended. I vaguely remember being told the information I was after wasn't public information so as to better protect the children involved with the C.A.S., and how the entry would be blocked out anyway. Maybe if I had gone to the courthouse in person things would have been different.

So many ideas and suggestions came from I.R.S., but eventually they stopped flowing and I stopped contacting them. I had reached the end of the line with them as I wasn't about to pay an hourly rate of fifteen dollars when I could continue on my own. They had taught me some new ways to examine the non-identifying information, so I didn't feel it was a total waste of my time or money. My last trimester involved countless specialist appointments. My Ob/Gyn in Sarnia still wanted me to continue with our regular visits along with the ones I had scheduled in London at the High-Risk Clinic. It was during this time, my doctors recommended I visit a nutritionist at St. Joseph's Hospital in London. Gestational diabetes was causing too much weight gain for the baby and me, so a diabetic diet was the first stage in treating this disease. Diabetes causes carbohydrates to turn into fat for the baby. The baby could end up gaining too much weight, which might hinder the delivery process. Darian had been delivered one week early and weighed a whopping nine pounds twelve ounces, so the potential for another large baby was imminent.

The dietician visually demonstrated proper quantities of food and we discussed a diet to follow so insulin could be avoided. She asked what my favourite food was and I quickly said ice cream. She allowed me a cup of ice cream each night before bed—my one pleasure—so my blood sugar levels remained stable during sleep. The diet worked and I continued to maintain a healthy weight until delivery.

Two weeks before my delivery date, blood tests showed my platelet count was decreasing at an alarming rate. I would unquestionably be delivering the baby in London. I knew this baby was going to be a planned delivery, but I was surprised when the specialist at the High-Risk Clinic suggested I could deliver my baby the following day. I agreed to be induced, based on my experience with delivering Darian. It had all worked out fine then, so I thought this time would be the same. Being in a hospital where they have the necessary equipment to control the circumstances was the best course of action for my high-risk deliveries.

We needed to be at the hospital in London for 7:30 a.m., and being an hour away, Jim and I decided Darian should sleep over somewhere. I quickly arranged for Darian to stay at Ben's house, as I knew he would have quite the adventure playing with Ben and his two brothers. He was pretty excited to be dropped off when we told him he would have a baby brother or sister sometime the next day. Sleep did not come easily for me that night as so many thoughts and worries went through my mind. It was almost as if I was lying awake listening for the alarm to go off so I wouldn't sleep in. I hoped a platelet transfusion was not needed and my baby was born with no complications. When morning finally came and the alarm went off, I was exhausted. I wondered how I could possibly deliver a baby in this state, so I prayed on the way to the hospital for strength to endure the labour and for a healthy baby.

Jason Robert Scott, our miracle baby, was born later that afternoon, with no complications. I believed God did answer my desperate prayers. I had been told my chances were zero percent of ever conceiving again and now here we were, holding this medical marvel. Jason weighed seven pounds thirteen ounces, clear proof my diet worked. He wasn't even close to being ten pounds like Darian had been. They had broken my water to induce labour, and it took nowhere near the amount of time to push him out as it did Darian. My platelet count was still a concern but I had not needed a transfusion. My platelet and sugar levels gradually returned to a more normal state postpartum, creating less worry for me and my doctors.

Darian had been an only child for six years. Jim and I gave him the honour of naming his little brother so he would feel proud, included, and important. At the time, he loved the show "Power Rangers" and the red one was his favourite. Jason was named after the red Power Ranger. I had thought of other possible names, but I knew Darian needed a connection with this baby for them to bond. This was just the beginning of their sibling relationship so I wanted to start it off on the right foot.

My little family was complete and small-town living seemed to suit us. Our three-bedroom home had a perfect sized backyard for the boys to run and explore in and it was located only a half-hour drive to Jim's workplace in Sarnia. It was the ideal place for us to raise our children with its low crime rate, rural school, and caring neighbours. To top things off, Jim and I both had extended family living nearby. All this made me feel safe and I knew my children would thrive living in Inwood.

But that safe feeling was threatened one day after I received a letter in the mail.

The first thing I noticed was there was no return address on the envelope. This seemed odd, as did the feel of the envelope itself. It felt too thin like it was missing its contents. It was addressed to "W Scott" and had my complete address handwritten on the front. This part seemed normal. When I opened it, there was nothing inside. Empty. Not a single scrap of paper. Could the sender just have forgotten to include the contents?

I was on my way to toss it in the garbage when something caught my eye. "LET IT GO" was handwritten on the inside of the envelope where the flap comes down.

Those three little words were all it took for my safe little world to feel threatened.

CHAPTER TWENTY-FOUR

REACHING AN IMPASSE

1997

After receiving the threatening letter, I waited almost a year before starting my investigation again. The letter had truly scared me at first. Obviously "LET IT GO" was a warning to stop looking for Dwayne. For me to STOP my search. I bet it was a response to my letter in the Reader to Reader column. My name and mailing address were attached to the column, and since Inwood was such a small village, it would not have taken long for them to ask around and find my residential address. But no harm had come to any of us, so as time passed I decided it was just an idle threat. And to be honest, a break from the search was also a good thing because having baby Jason to take care of was a full-time job. He seemed not to sleep very much that first year, so most days I felt sleep-deprived.

This took a toll on me. I lost weight, felt depressed, and struggled to cope. When Jason was six months old, I developed mastitis (a breast infection), so I had to stop nursing due to the antibiotics I was prescribed. Having Jason on a bottle meant Jim could feed him too. This turned out to be a great relief for me—I finally started getting some sleep—and Jim became closer to Jason during their special feeding times. Before long, Jason was able to sleep through the night.

But even after I was getting enough sleep I remained gloomy and downcast. It dragged on too long to be baby blues. My family doctor finally diagnosed me with depression and I was put back on antidepressants. My depression made it difficult to be the mom and wife I had hoped to be. I had the family I had always dreamed of and it was heartbreaking to have to force myself out of bed to care for my two beautiful boys and loving husband. I just felt so tired.

Overcoming depression is never easy. It takes a lot of positivity: positive thinking, positive talking, and positive people. My sister-in-law Barb was someone I could turn to for positivity. When I lost Alaric, I visited her old farmhouse on a dirt sideroad for a day of talking, eating her delicious soup, and learning how to purl so I could knit four-needle socks. Barb's house always smelled of rotten eggs because of the sulphur water, but the smokey smell of the wood stove masked it. She supported me through many sad days with her humour, food, and positive thinking. This time was no different.

Barb had moved to another home, just as cozy, but thankfully no rotten egg smell this time, or woodstove for that matter. I brought Jason with me and while she played with and loved him up, we talked. She had been through tough times herself, growing up in a home where her parents ended up divorcing. There were seven kids in their family. They endured an abusive, alcoholic mother who was left to care for them, while their dad was away working as a long haul truck driver. All that along with her difficulties in marriage and raising a family, it was incredible Barb remained such a positive person. But she remained strong and steadfast in her beliefs and became a wonderful confidant and mentor for me. I never wanted our visits to end.

With the help of medication, positive people, knitting, love for my boys and husband, and the drive to look for Dwayne, I slowly crawled out of the awful deep dark hole I had been trapped in. After several months, I found myself wanting to go outside for walks, knit four-needle socks, go on dates with Jim, play on the floor with my kids and read them bedtime stories, and socialize with friends and family. My goal had been to only be on the antidepressants for a short time, and it ended up only being for about a year. I am still proud of the hard work I did to come back to myself. As soon as I was healthy, my thoughts returned to Dwayne. As I mentioned, nothing ever came of the "LET IT GO" threat. So really, all it did was make me more determined. To whoever the person was behind that pathetic attempt to scare me, I triumphantly yelled into the air, "Try and stop me!"

Back on track, my first call was to 1-800-US SEARCH. After seeing a commercial for this service on TV I knew I had to check it out. I reached voicemail, but after waiting three days with no reply I called them back. They required a current name and birthdate to be of any further assistance. I had neither of those, so I scratched that lead off my list.

Next an ad for "Adoptees-Birth Parents" caught my eye while I was browsing through the announcements section of our free weekly paper. I cut out the ad and put it aside to look into the following week. Also, I learned Parent Finders of Sarnia was going to have an information booth at the mall where I had an upcoming dental appointment. What great timing! On the day of my appointment, I grabbed Dwayne's file and headed out.

After finishing up at the dentist's office, I headed over to the booth with anticipation of a new lead. The representative and I discussed registering with Parent Finders and how attending their meetings in Sarnia could put me in touch with people who could help me with my search. The group consisted of individuals who had been successful with their searches and ones who were still looking. But joining the Parent Finders group and paying their registration fee wasn't something I felt ready for. Also, I didn't feel emotionally equipped to share my personal story with such a large group of strangers. So I headed home feeling disappointed about another dead end. To add more disappointment, I learned my contact person at the C.A.S. had been changed. Thinking back to our last conversation where I had pushed for more information than they were allowed to share, I wondered if our good rapport had been damaged and this was how she handled it. I left a message for the new worker to contact me and heard back a few days later. I introduced myself, gave her some history as to why I was searching for Dwayne, and asked if there were any new updates to my file. Unfortunately, there were none. This worker seemed pleasant and I immediately noticed something different about her. Maybe because she was new to my case, those old feelings of hope resurfaced. When she recommended a private investigator who had success with finding adoptees, I jumped at the opportunity. The hourly fees of a private investigator could be costly, but I figured a phone consultation couldn't hurt. After writing down the name and number, she wished me luck and we ended our conversation.

Right away I called the private investigator's office. "Hello, Ms. Patterson. My name is Wendy Scott and you were highly recommended by someone I'm working with at the C.A.S." I gave her the name of my contact person and then proceeded when she confirmed that she knew her. I provided a brief history of my story and what I had accomplished so far. "I'm looking for my half-brother and have received the non-identifying information."

"That's great Wendy. How can I help you?" she asked politely.

"First of all, I want to be honest with you. I can't afford to pay someone an hourly fee to investigate for me, but I'd truly appreciate some ideas on how I can use the information I have. I need some fresh eyes on the case," I openly replied.

She hesitated. Silence. Then said, "I don't usually do this but maybe we can talk a bit further. I won't charge you, but together we can decide on your next course of action."

Again I was astounded by the generosity of strangers. It was easy to like this woman.

"So tell me about the adoptive parents," she began, "What were their occupations?"

"The father was a beverage company salesman and the mother was a nurse," I answered.

"Let me think," she said.

I waited patiently through the silence, wondering what she could extract from this clue.

"Do you know the age of the adoptive mother?" she inquired.

"Yes, I do. She was twenty-seven at the time of the adoption." I was puzzled as to why this mattered.

"Have you tried requesting a list of graduates from

the archives at Victoria Hospital in London? You can probably guess her graduating year based on her age."

This was not something I had thought of. I had requested employee records from another hospital, where I assumed she could have found employment. I had also asked Parent Finders about grad nursing books, but they did not think any books like that existed.

"No. I haven't thought of this. Thanks so much. I'll look into it," I exclaimed.

She wished me luck, I thanked her again, and then we said our goodbyes.

Days later, I called for the list of graduates, asking that it range from 1957-1967. This way, I could cover a longer period, allowing no room for errors. The list arrived in the mail within a few days. I couldn't wait to open it and start trying to match the names up with my list of adoptive parents.

The list of nursing school graduates contained both maiden and married (if applicable) names and addresses. I had wondered how I would go about determining their marital status at the time of graduation. After further research, it was my understanding nurses had to notify the College of Nurses of any important changes to remain current and in good standing. This made things a lot easier for me.

Although the list covered ten years, I homed in on 1959 to 1961 as her approximate graduation years. I guessed her birthdate was around 1940 if she was twenty-eight in 1968. Then I added twenty years (assuming she was eighteen at high school graduation plus two more years for nursing college) to 1940 to determine her age as a nursing grad, taking it to 1960. I also included one year before and after 1960 to allow some leeway in my calculations.

I looked at my list, composed through hours of intense research using microfiche, and I cross-referenced it to the list of nursing grads, starting in 1959. About halfway through 1959 there was a match. I stared in awe, as the names jumped off the page at me, and my heart pounded. Back and forth from name to name, I studied them, thinking this just could not be possible. "I may have found Dwayne," I thought. Now if only he or his adoptive family were still living in London this mystery would soon be solved.

My immediate thought was to contact London Parent Finders to see if they had this person or family in their registry. When I didn't get a reply from them within a few days, I called my new contact person at the C.A.S. and left her a message, inquiring if I had the right family. It was worth a shot and I had nothing to lose. I was so sure that I had broken the case thanks to my detective skills. No reply came from either source, so after a month of waiting I turned to Plan B. I called the London Public Library.

This surely had to be the right family as everything matched up perfectly. The mother was on my list of nursing graduates and she and her spouse had placed a birth announcement in the paper. The words in the announcement indicated their "chosen son" was welcomed into their family around the time Dwayne had been adopted. Now all I had left to do was confirm the father was a beverage company salesman. How hard could that be? It turned out the city directory at the library did have a listing for this couple in 1968, but the father's occupation was not listed as a beverage company salesman. It was listed as a professor at a university. There was no current telephone listing for either the couple or the son, and 411 confirmed the same. They were nowhere to be found within the London area.

I investigated two other possibilities from the list of grads and came up with a big fat zero ... nothing. Just when I had my hopes up, my dreams of finding Dwayne were dashed. My search had reached yet another impasse.

"Together Again" read the headline on the Saturday edition of *The Observer*. Even though Sarnia was small it had its own newspaper that I occasionally purchased for the puzzles and comics. I loved doing the Jumble where you have to unscramble the letters to form a word and then unscramble the circled letters to form another word or phrase. But this time the headline caught my eye and I was inspired by what I read. A mother had found her adopted daughter through the Adoption Disclosure Registry. Since they had both registered, they were matched up and reunited. The mother explained in the article that she felt a sense of loss, grief, anxiety, guilt, fear, and shame after giving her daughter up for adoption. Much like Nancy, she had been very young when she found herself pregnant and didn't have many options.

This mother, an adult now, was involved in Sarnia Parent Finders. This group kept turning up during my search, so I pondered whether it was time to give them a whirl and enlist their help. It would mean paying a fee to join the group, but even more I would have to share my story in person, opening myself up to vulnerability.

Up to that point, I had been on the expedition mainly by myself. I had only been talking on the phone to people, not seeing many in person. I had mastered any anxieties or fears by using my trusty notes to practice what I was going to say beforehand. In person would be a whole other story. The information I had received from people was like stepping stones that had brought me to where I was. I had come a long way, but there was still farther to go. I needed more stepping stones and I wasn't going to find them on my own. Was Sarnia Parent Finders the answer? Would they offer more stepping stones for my journey or would the lead just dissolve into tiny grains of sand, disappearing between my fingers?

CHAPTER TWENTY-FIVE

FAMILY, FRIENDS, AND FRESH LEADS

1999

Seasons came and went, and before I knew it two years had passed by and I was no further in my search for Dwayne. When you have a young family, life becomes something of a blur. And really, who could blame me for getting frustrated with what was feeling more and more like a pointless search?

Wintertime for us promised cold temperatures that produced plenty of snow for building forts and snowmen and covered hills for tobogganing and skiing. At the time, we had a neighbour who built an outdoor skating rink, equipped with nets, make-shift boards, spotlights, a warm campfire, and a Zamboni he had invented himself. This provided a popular spot for many children and adults to practice their skating and stickhandling skills. A former NHL player living in the neighbourhood would even visit the rink on occasion.

Like many other Canadian families, we were heavily involved in Canada's most popular winter sport, hockey. With Darian registered in minor hockey, we had the privilege of spending most of our waking hours in cold arenas and dishing out our hard-earned money on expensive hockey equipment, hotel rooms, gas for our vehicle, and eating out. This was necessary for Darian's out of town hockey tournaments once he was chosen for the travel team. That formal process involved try-outs, leaving disappointed little boys and girls feeling left out and inadequate. Darian had this happen to him once but handled the rejection much better than Jim or me.

So after packing our suitcases and Darian's hockey gear, we would battle the icy, snow-covered roads, often in blizzard conditions, to make our way to a weekend tournament. Many weekends you would find us in some far-off city, surrounded by various teams and their hockey families. I never could conform to this way of life, or the freezing arenas. Jason did though. He loved going anywhere with his big brother. He adored and looked up to Darian.

Hockey can become quite a political sport, with parents fighting over equal ice time and fair treatment for their child. There were times when Jim's efforts to support his son would cause friction with the coach and even the other parents. This always left me feeling uncomfortable, as I hated conflict. But since I loved being with my little family and seeing Darian skate effortlessly down the ice to score the winning goal, I put my feelings aside and continued year after year to struggle through each hockey season. I did it for Darian and the betterment of my family.

In summertime, we ventured on plenty of camping trips. We mostly camped in Ontario, but later when the boys were older we visited Cedar Point in Ohio, United States. First, we had a motorhome and next a tent trailer. The motorhome was already set up, so there was not a lot to do except pack and go. It was so old it had an eight-track tape player. When explaining the age of our motorhome to people, all we had to say was that it had the original eight-track player and that pretty much said it all. It was always good for a laugh. We sold the motorhome because every time we left our campsite to drive into town our hoses and firewood would be gone when we returned. People thought when they didn't see the motorhome anymore we had checked out of the campground, so they helped themselves to our things. The tent trailer was purchased brand new, and we felt very fortunate to own such a luxury. It was fairly easy to pack but took a little work to set up.

One time when Jim was setting up the trailer, the boys and I decided to go for a hike. When we first saw Cyprus Lake, it looked like we could make it around in about a half-hour. Shortly after setting off, though, I warned the boys we'd miscalculated and that we should turn back as our little hike was going to take a lot longer than planned. Darian and Jason both argued it wouldn't be that long, so I wondered if this could be a teaching moment. We didn't have cell phones back then, so if something were to happen we were on our own.

We kept going, and after a half-hour Darian finally realized that Mom could be right. Jason's little legs were getting tired, so both Darian and I took turns carrying him. At one point we heard and saw something slither quickly across the trail but just figured it was a common garter snake. It took us more than an hour to make it around the lake and we all learned to be a better judge of distance. Later on during our vacation, we saw a sign warning that Cyprus Lake had rattlesnakes and to be cautious. Another lesson learned. We should have become more knowledgeable of the wildlife in the area before heading out for a hike.

And what about my search for Dwayne? Two years pass quickly when you are busy raising a family. Plus I had also lost interest in my search. All the dead ends had caused me so much frustration that I gave up. Each new clue had left me in anticipation of finding Dwayne and then I would be left feeling disappointed when the lead went nowhere. It felt similar to a slow motion rollercoaster ride, a never-ending loop, going up and down, and around and around. There seemed to be no end in sight.

Suddenly I realized I had never followed up on the Sarnia Parent Finders group suggestion. Maybe I was ready to get out of my comfort zone. After looking through my file, I found the information I had filed away for future use. Their monthly meetings were held every third Monday, and so I planned to attend the next one. I hoped they would be able to make some suggestions and help me find my half-brother. My file was ready to go so all I had to do was wait for Monday.

I attended the meeting in Sarnia that Monday night, but I was on edge the whole time. My script, the one I had previously used on the telephone, was not going to work at in-person meetings. I would have to wing it when the time came for me to speak. All the people there seemed to be birth parents or adoptees searching for their loved ones. Since I was only a half-sibling, I worried the other attendees may think my search wasn't as important as theirs.

For the most part, I just listened. I wrote down any new ways of searching they discussed and I was given a search buddy. That evening, he and I talked about what I had already done and he suggested I place ads in newspapers, which of course would cost money. I graciously accepted an information package that I could examine further at home. Leaving the meeting that night, I was overwhelmed by the ample list of ideas I had not known about. One way to search is through baptismal records, which I knew nothing about, so I decided to pay a visit to some women who did.

Miss Barber, Dorothy, and Jean had not only cared for me as a young child, but also they had become a second set of grandmothers to my children. They spoiled them at Christmas and always made sure to connect with us throughout the year. We visited often so they could see the boys growing up. At their house, you always sat around the kitchen table to eat and visit. The home-cooked food was never-ending, along with the enjoyable conversations. There was always lots to talk about. The ladies were unique and I loved each one for different reasons. They were known in Arkona as The Golden Girls.

My visit this time was about my search. They had been supportive and knew what I was doing, so asking for their help made sense. Two of the ladies were ministers and would have performed many baptisms. I asked them about how records would be kept for these, and if it would be possible for me to track down Dwayne using this method.

They all agreed it would be difficult. Since I didn't know what branch of Protestant faith Dwayne was, I didn't have a church to start with. There were a lot of churches in London, so I would have had to visit each one and ask to look at their records. Pentecostals believe in baptisms for adults and dedications for babies. This added another dimension to my already confused state. In the end, I decided to set that idea aside.

It was time again to check for updates at the C.A.S., so I phoned my contact person. Parent Finders in Sarnia had suggested three new questions for me to ask about Dwayne:

1. Is he alive or dead?

2. Does he know he's adopted?

3. Has he ever contacted them?

After a month of trying to connect with my contact person, I finally reached her. It was difficult for me to imagine how she was so busy that she couldn't return my call, so I was persistent. The persistence paid off. She replied to all three of my questions.

1. If Dwayne was dead, she would have contacted me.

2. Most people know they are adopted nowadays.

3. If he had ever contacted them, she would have referred him to the Adoption Disclosure Registry.

It was a relief to know that Dwayne must be alive. I couldn't imagine wasting my time searching for someone who had passed on. It had been well worth the wait to hear that answer. The other two answers did not provide me with any new information, but I was still thankful for her cooperation.

Spring of 2000

Our backyards in Inwood all joined up to one another. No fences separated the properties, only gardens, shrubs, and trees. If a neighbour was outside hanging clothes, cutting grass, gardening, sitting on their deck, or playing with their children, it was common practice to be neighbourly and wave or start a conversation. Our neighbour, Linda, kitty-corner to us, had an umbrella clothesline and would regularly hang her clothes outside to dry.

One day, while Jason and I were outside at the sandbox, I spotted Linda hanging her clothes. Since Jason was engrossed in building roads in the sand for his dinky toys, I started chatting with Linda. After talking about the beautiful day, she casually asked what was new. I, of course, was excited to tell her of my search for Dwayne. I was so thankful just to have another adult to talk to, and I appreciated her valuable time. She listened intently, and then shared that she had a friend who had found her birth parent. When I confessed my initial concern about the "LET IT GO" warning, she shared that her friend had received the exact same envelope! We both agreed it must have been some crusader trying to scare people away from finding their loved ones.

I asked Linda how her friend had found her birth parent, and she said a man named Lynn Clark had helped in the search. He lived in Chatham at the time, which was about an hour from Inwood. He had been retired for many years, and his spare time was spent helping people find loved ones. Lynn did this out of the goodness of his heart. My interest piqued at this point, and I decided to be brave and just ask her if she could find out his contact information. She wasn't sure if he would offer his help, but said she would ask her friend for me.

Computer searches and using the internet were still fairly new for me at this time, but I quickly learned how to look up adoption websites. And so I began hopping from site to site, each one with possible links to another site. I finally ended up at Barrie Parent Finders. What I recall was a free registry and searchable database, meaning no fee to use it. It was all done online with no paperwork involved. This was simple and seemed to be the most efficient way to register. After deciding it was a legitimate group, I settled into my computer chair and started entering my and Dwayne's information. After I was done, I prayed that if I was meant to find Dwayne he would be in their database.

I checked and rechecked but did not find a single thing. He must not have registered, which could mean he was not looking or was just unaware of the site. If for some reason he did register, the site manager would be alerted and then contact me. Having up-to-date information was crucial for a match.

Sometimes in life we do things, and unknowingly they lead to something else. Our actions can cause a chain reaction. At that particular moment, it seemed futile to register with Barrie Parent Finders. Little did I know doing this it would provide another missing piece to the puzzle. But we'll get to that later.

My neighbour acted quickly. After only a few days Linda had contacted her friend and learned Lynn was open to talking to me, although he promised nothing. At least I now had his phone number. Linda had proven herself to be a great friend. I prepared my notes before calling Lynn. To convince him to help, I knew I would have to include all events leading up to my search, plus the research I had completed along the way. I did not leave out a single event. I started at the beginning: the death of my father. I hoped and prayed it would be good enough to persuade Lynn to help.

Since this could be my last hope of ever finding Dwayne, I knew it had better be convincing.

CHAPTER TWENTY-SIX

SHERLOCK AND WATSON

May 2000

By late spring of 2000, I could not believe how fast my kids were growing up. Darian was ten, and Jason was almost four which meant he would be starting school in the fall. He couldn't wait to ride the big yellow school bus with his older brother. Jason would also be enrolled in hockey, so I'd get to have double the fun in freezing arenas. I tried convincing myself I was lucky to have both boys busy playing hockey instead of getting into trouble. In truth, I think it did help keep them on track both mentally and physically. And if they were happy so was I.

Thoughts of starting up my home daycare again full time were put aside. I was asked to care for a little girl named Georgie a few days a week, and I gladly accepted.

This was a nice compromise. She was a year younger than Jason and made the perfect playmate. They got along extremely well so it was a joy having her with us. Just like Jason admired his big brother Darian, Georgie relished every moment with Jason. Once again, I found myself consumed with creating fun activities. My fondest memory with these sweet children was when we made crowns out of huge colourful fall leaves. We joined them all together very carefully and I placed the crowns on their heads. Georgie grinned from ear to ear when I took her picture. What an angel she was with her blonde curls and round, cherubic face.

The days without Georgie, I stared at Lynn's phone number and debated calling him. I asked myself what I would do if he decided not to help me, and I didn't like my answer. I would probably give up looking altogether. This was my last resort. My search was at a stalemate unless I wanted to put serious cash into hiring a private investigator. I went with the cheaper option and called Lynn.

I reviewed the notes I had made when I first got his number and then dialled. He answered after a few rings and I introduced myself. He had been expecting my call, as Linda's friend had given him a bit of background information about me. Lynn was a very pleasant man and I guessed him to be well into his retirement years. He listened closely while I read every detail from my notes, trying not to overlook anything. I stressed how important it was for me to find Dwayne and how much I needed his experience and expertise to carry through with my search.

There was no need to worry. After hearing my case, Lynn offered his assistance. I was to mail him the non-identifying information along with any other registrations, lists, or leads I had tried to follow up with. We would collaboratively use my leads and his knowledge of searching so no time was wasted on duplicated ideas or information. When I asked him how much this was all going to cost me, he said not a penny. He would not accept money, as he was taking on my case to help me, not to make a profit. I really admired Lynn for that.

A week later, after receiving and reviewing the information, Lynn called me. I could already tell he was a man who got things done. And he knew his stuff. He suggested writing a short form letter to all the nursing grads on the 1960-1961 Alumnae list of nurses. The list I had would be up to date because as I explained in an earlier chapter, nurses had to notify the College of Nurses of any important changes to remain current and in good standing. The list contained both maiden and married names plus their address. His second suggestion was to do some more digging into the London city directories, but adding a new angle. He wanted to compare the 1967 and 1968 London city directories against the Alumnae list. He chose these dates based on the non-identifying information report that revealed Dwayne was put up for adoption in 1967 and the final adoption order was signed in 1968. The report also stated that his adoptive mother was 28 years old at the time of the adoption in 1968. This means she would have been born in 1940 and would have graduated from nursing school around 1960-1961. I was really excited to see what might come from bringing all of this research together.

The easiest route, I felt, was to use the London city directories and compare them to the Alumnae list. A gut instinct, intuition, or whatever you want to call it, kept drawing me time and time again to these resources at the library. Writing the form letter to all the grads could be our Plan B. Lynn said it would be most beneficial if we could access these directories in person. He had a medical appointment in London in about a month and would be more than happy to visit the library while there. He said it would be easier to skim and scan each directory in person while trying to find a match rather than calling and asking for assistance over the phone.

During the month-long wait, another lead came in. My sister Wanda noticed a very handsome gentleman in her local newspaper and thought he looked like our dad. He had worked as an investment advisor for a company in London. After receiving the picture, I closely inspected it. The man, Bob, looked to be thirty-something which would coincide with Dwayne's age. His jet black hair, high forehead, and large chin were similar to that of my dad. I pulled out the photo album to compare the newspaper photo with my dad's old black and white photos. The photos I treasured of my dad were only ever printed in black and white. That was unfortunate because a coloured photo would have enhanced his dark good looks and captured his mischievous hazel eyes.

Bob absolutely resembled my dad, and to confirm my earlier suspicions, I checked the list of nursing grads. His last name was somewhat uncommon and I thought I remembered seeing it on the list. I immediately found it. There was a possibility that a nursing grad named Jean was his adoptive mother. Ross was listed as her husband and they resided in Kitchener, Ontario at the time the list was printed. Kitchener is only about one hour away from London. With the close proximity, the chances of this couple moving from one city to the other was highly possible. They could have also lived in Kitchener and adopted out of London. I considered just cold calling Bob using the number from the ad. First, though, I wanted to check with my new partner Lynn to see what he thought. Does Sherlock ever solve a case without involving Watson?

I was so disappointed when Lynn's answering machine picked up. "This isn't the time to be away, Lynn!" I thought. I could hardly refrain from calling the number in the ad. I remembered how some adoptees do not know their history and since this wasn't something for me to tell, I somehow stopped myself from calling.

While impatiently waiting, I followed up on another lead from a few months back. While at a family gathering,

I had casually mentioned my search for Dwayne to a family member. He hesitantly shared that he may have an idea of who the adoptive parents could be but didn't want to give me any more information. He said to leave it with him. His body language, facial expression, and tone of voice led me to believe I should drop it. I filed the conversation away, but now months later I called him in hopes he would be more open on the phone. He explained his lead was only a hunch and he would not share any names unless he knew for certain it wasn't going to upset anyone. We agreed I'd send him the list of names Lynn compiled during his visit to the London library. He said he would call me if the name he had in mind showed up on the list. After I hung up the phone, I knew I would not revisit this lead.

Besides the "LET IT GO" incident, I had met no opposition during my search, only helpful people with useful information. This particular phone call, though, had me wondering if I should follow through with my mission. The thought of creating a bad situation or hurting anyone's feelings by bringing up the past wasn't something I wanted to do. For a fleeting moment, I let one man's negativity get the best of me. I watched as a few of the carefully placed stepping stones vanished from beneath my feet. My path forward and my spirits were shattered. How to move on from this?

Before long, though, the way forward revealed itself with a simple ring of the phone. Lynn called me back and I was excited to share my lead about the newspaper ad guy. He agreed it sounded promising. Lynn always offered support and good advice. I marvelled at his thought process. He said to contact Jean or Ross, the possible adoptive parents of Bob. We discussed how I should check both London and Kitchener telephone and city directories. He also added, "If they aren't who you are looking for, ask Jean if she remembers any other graduates who may have adopted during our time frame. You just never know, Wendy. It can't hurt to ask." Lynn always knew what to say and exuded confidence. That is why we were such a good fit. I believed in him.

Now to do my part. First I called the Kitchener Public Library and asked for the 1967 city directory listing for Ross and Jean. It listed Ross as a salesman. When I heard that my heart started palpitating and my palms were sweaty. My head was swimming with thoughts of how this could be it ... I had finally found Dwayne. I truly felt this was the end of my long journey. I just needed a current telephone listing, so once I had regained my composure I asked for any listings on these individuals, and I received two.

Shot down again. After calling both listings, I learned they were not the right people. My rehearsed speech about the reason for my call was improving, though, and I could almost pull it off without notes. Unfortunately, I'd had lots of opportunity to practice. After hanging up from these two calls, I quickly regained momentum based on what Lynn and I had discussed. Maybe they were living in London, so I called 411 and asked for current telephone listings in London. This time there were three listings.

One call, two calls, three calls. Nothing. All were dead ends.

I decided to make it four calls because really, what did I have to lose? If Bob did or didn't know he was adopted had no bearing on me at this point. I had to know if he was Dwayne. He answered and I started rattling off my usual dialogue, inserting an occasional "Ummm … " when stumped for anything else to say. My age estimation had not been too far off, but it was not a match. Bob's birthday was in April 1971 and Dwayne had been born in 1967—not even close. Darn. I had thought this one was the jackpot.

There is a saying about leaving no stone unturned. In my particular case, it felt like all the stones along my path had been turned but revealed nothing. And I couldn't place another one down to move any further. My foot was left dangling in mid-air, ready to step down but nothing was there. But I didn't allow myself to get too worried. I felt certain my trusty partner Watson would help lay that next stone when he visited the London Public Library.

June 11, 2000

On Sunday, Lynn called to see if I had any updates and

to remind me of his trip to London the next day. I shared my week's worth of dead ends and he said not to worry. He would visit the London Public Library and return with some new leads. We would keep trying.

I knew Lynn's trip to London was for a medical appointment and hoped it was not for anything too serious. We never really discussed our personal lives ... we just got down to business. And our business was finding Dwayne.

I wished him luck and safe travels. His day would be full, with at least one hour from Chatham to London, and who knew how long his appointment would be. If he was going all the way to London, chances were it was to see a specialist. Specialist appointments, in particular, can run behind by as much as an hour. On top of all that, Lynn would need to eat lunch somewhere and then hopefully still have time left to visit the library.

June 12, 2000

The next evening, Lynn called a little after nine. I hardly believed he could get back to me so soon. He must have just gotten in the door from his trip to London and wanted to share something.

"Wendy. It's Lynn. I think we may have a lead. Do you have a pen and paper?" Just like Lynn ... no time for idle chatter.

"Yes, Lynn. Go ahead," I answered breathlessly. This could be it.

"So I had a very successful day in London. I visited

the library after my appointment and came up with a few leads. I'll give you the first one which sounds the most promising, and if it's not it we'll move on to the next." Lynn dictated the names of two people as well as their current address and phone number. Boom. Just like that, he had everything. Plus he had a backup just in case this one didn't work out. The names were of potential adoptive parents and they lived in London. He had found them using the London city directory and grad list.

"Let me know how you make out, Wendy."

"Of course, Lynn. I hope we got it this time. Thanks again for helping me out with all this. Are you sure I can't offer you some kind of compensation? I know the phone calls are long-distance, so at least let me pay you for those?" I somehow didn't feel right taking this man's time without giving him something in return.

"I don't mind at all. Don't worry about the calls. And I was going to London anyway. I just want to help you find Dwayne." Lynn ended our call and I just sat there stunned by all that Lynn had accomplished in such a short period of time. Since our call happened so late, I would have to wait until the next day to find out if this was the end of my search.

The number of phone calls made in my search for Dwayne seemed to be endless. Just when I thought there wouldn't be any more, there was. "Please, let this be the last one," I prayed before bed that night. "Dear God, if I can find him then I'll be at peace. Amen."

June 13, 2000

I called the number Lynn gave me and spoke with Joanne. She said they weren't the couple I was looking for. She took my name and number in case she remembered any nursing graduates who might have adopted around 1968.

During our call, I used the term "adopted" instead of "loved one" or "family member." Some of the organizations I had dealt with had warned me against using the term "adopted." They had said it would scare people off and they wouldn't want to cooperate. But I always used the term when contacting hopeful candidates because I felt it was a more honest approach. All of the cooperation and polite responses I had received during my search proved to me I had made the right decision.

June 14, 2000

The next day, Lynn and I touched base. We had made it our routine to keep in touch so any new leads remained fresh and current. I was energized by Lynn's enthusiasm and didn't have time to sit around and sulk when leads ended in dead ends. Since the first couple hadn't panned out, we moved on to the backup. I remember thinking that Watson and I would solve this mystery even if it took forever. Somehow, he would always come up with more clues. It seemed like the ideas would keep flowing from

Lynn, no matter what. We would always have something to fall back on.

He then gave me the information on the other possible couple. When he said their last name, I had to ask him to repeat it.

He repeated the name "Hawkins" and I fell silent.

CHAPTER TWENTY-SEVEN

WHAT'S IN A NAME?

June 14, 2000

"Please tell me you are joking, Lynn!" I exclaimed.

"No Wendy. I'm not joking. Why?" Lynn had no idea of what he was suggesting with the surname Hawkins.

"Lynn. Hawkins is my maiden name and it would have been Dwayne's last name if Nancy and my dad had been married. Do you think that would even be possible? What are the odds of that happening?" I asked.

"So let me get this straight. Your dad's surname was Hawkins?" I could hear the surprise in Lynn's voice.

"Yup. That's what makes this just too weird and impossible." It was out of the question for me to even think that this could be a lead, but Lynn convinced me otherwise.

"Wendy. It's still a valid lead. Let me tell you why," Lynn assured me.

"You can try, but I just can't believe it." He would have to offer some very compelling evidence to change my mind.

"When I researched this couple, I had a good feeling so I really went in-depth with my search in the city directories. Starting in 1962, I followed the father's work history until 1970 where I found what I was looking for. The father, Kenneth Hawkins, had been employed by Home Juice Company ... and guess what he was?" Lynn asked.

"A salesman," I jokingly replied.

"Right on, Wendy. He was a salesman, which ties in with the non-identifying info about the adopted father being a beverage company salesman. Juice definitely constitutes a beverage!" Lynn added.

"Okay, Lynn. That is more than what I have come up with so far. And was the wife a nurse on that list I gave you?" I would need this match to convince me there might be something to this.

"Yes. Joyce Hawkins (nee Roberts) was on the list. So both parents match up with the non-identifying information, Wendy. What do you think?" Lynn had all his bases covered and I had nowhere left to run.

"You got me, Lynn. I have no choice but to follow up. I bet you have a current phone number too," I laughed.

"Of course I do. Here it is." Lynn proceeded to

give me the current telephone number of Kenneth and Joyce Hawkins.

As I wrote it down, my thoughts turned to this kind and caring man who had so generously offered his time and effort into helping me, a stranger.

"Lynn, I do hope we have it right this time. If it happens to be Dwayne, it would be a total miracle. His last name at birth should have been Hawkins. Thank you so much for your help." My voice shook with emotion as we said our goodbyes. We left it at I would try calling the next day to give me time to regroup.

When Jim got home from work, I shared my news. Like me, he just didn't think it was possible. The chances were one in a million of Dwayne ending up with the same name as his dad and I. We agreed I should rule it out by calling the next day. Just like any good detective, I wanted to leave no stone unturned.

June 15, 2000

After a fitful night's sleep, I woke exhausted but ready to place the call. Darian had school and Georgie was at her Grandma's, so I only had Jason to contend with. After breakfast, I settled him into an activity and started to get prepared. Since this would be another cold call to a stranger, I wrote down, in point form, everything I wanted to say. I'd explain that I'm doing some family research and am looking for a married couple who lived in London in 1968. The husband had been a beverage company salesman and the wife a nurse. The couple had adopted a little boy, born on June 15, 1967, from the London C.A.S. Dwayne had been his given name at birth and he was my half-brother.

Cold calling strangers was still hard even though I had placed so many calls over the past seven years in hopes of finding Dwayne. Having Lynn as my partner, though, made me feel accountable to someone besides myself. It changed things somehow. I needed to report the outcome of the call to Lynn, so I forged ahead, stubborn and determined.

I tried the phone number and got an answering machine. After all that build up! But at least the machine confirmed I had the right household ... so that was promising. I didn't leave a message because these people had no clue who I was and I wouldn't know what to say anyway. I would try again later.

I was curious to know if there was a listing for a Dwayne or a D. Hawkins in London, so I called 411. There was one listing in London so I copied it down. My intent was not to contact Dwayne at this time, but I was curious and could use the information as backup if needed. It never hurt to have a Plan B and just knowing this phone number might be Dwayne's made him seem more real than ever before.

Usually, when I had the nerve to place calls and no one answered the first time it was hard to mentally prepare myself to try again. I would overthink it so much that eventually anxiety overcame my confidence. Reaffirming to myself the need to find Dwayne and the purpose behind my search eventually convinced me to keep going. My stubborn redhead side was where I felt the best mentally but I often struggled to get there. When I was there, anything was possible.

With dinner done and Jim watching the kids play hockey in the laneway while he puttered in the garage, it was time to try again. No more excuses. So many thoughts went through my head as I picked up the receiver. I prayed for guidance and then started to dial.

"Hello?" the woman on the other end answered.

"Hi. Is this Joyce Hawkins?" I asked.

"Yes, it is. Who's calling?" she replied.

"My name is Wendy Scott. You don't know me, but I'm doing some family research to help find a family member of mine. I was wondering if you would be willing to help me?"

" Sure. Go on, Wendy. I'm just not sure what it has to do with me or how I can help."

"Joyce, I'm looking for my half-brother who was adopted by a family in London. The father was a beverage company salesman and the mother a nurse. Could I possibly have the right family?"

After a moment of silence she replied, "I'm not sure. Can you please give me more information? Do you have any siblings?"

"Yes, sure. I have two sisters. I'm the middle child. I'd

also like to add I've been looking for Dwayne, his given name at birth, for about seven years and would love to find him."

"Wendy. Leave this with me." She paused for a moment and then added, "Can you give me your phone number?"

"Sure." I recited my phone number to Joyce and was left feeling unsure as to what had just happened.

Since she hadn't said yes or no about the possibility of them being the right couple, I felt a bit dumbfounded. The call to Joyce had been very different from the other cold calls. I hadn't received a definite answer.

We ended our conversation, but since I hadn't felt comfortable asking her what day she would call back it was all left up in the air. "She may never even call me back," I thought.

That same week, I got an offer to take a different direction in my career. Since my kind, caring, and empathetic nature shone through while caring for my daycare children, Elizabeth, Georgie's mom, asked me if I would like to work for St. Francis Advocates—a social service agency providing care to persons with autism or developmental disabilities. In her role as an administrator with the organization, she knew they needed extra staff. She asked if I would be interested in working as a casual call-in residential counsellor. I knew very little about the job requirements at the time, so I had been a little hesitant to accept. But since it would mean extra income for our family and I could continue caring for Georgie, as most call-ins were evenings and weekends, I decided to give it a try.

My role at St. Francis was a real learning curve for me, but it was soon evident why my life turned onto this particular road. I loved learning about this special population and the different ways I could help their day be awesome. Differences in moods and behaviours scared me at first, but once I got to know each resident as an individual, I learned to appreciate and accept what made each person unique. Having a good sense of humour, developing trust, earning respect, and being prepared for anything were key to success at this job. This role paved the way for my new career supporting individuals with special needs. Many other job opportunities would come my way in the future, each teaching me more valuable skills to best support and advocate for these exceptional individuals.

June 18, 2000 - Father's Day

Every Father's Day our little family mostly celebrated at home. Jim was on call 24/7 and worked a half-hour away in Sarnia. He appreciated just being at home with us and having a nice quiet day. This particular one was no different. The plan was for Jim to BBQ steak for supper and I was in charge of the salads and dessert.

I stay away from the BBQ as much as possible as it's really never been my thing. There is just way too much fussing. I like a recipe you can whip together, throw in the oven, set the temperature and timer, and go do something else until it's done. I hate standing around a hot smokey BBQ. All you do is poke, turn, wipe your eyes thanks to the smoke, cough, check the meat, and repeat.

Those special Father's Days spent with my boys and Jim were, at least at first, very peculiar. Growing up without a father, I had only ever spent the day with my mom, sisters, and Grandma. It would be similar to any other Sunday, where we attended church in the morning and evening and rested in the afternoon. Our main meal was at lunch and usually consisted of pot roast with all the fixings. Some families without fathers at least had a grandfather or other male figure to fill those shoes. This did not happen in my case.

When Jim and I had children and started celebrating Father's Day, it took a little bit for me to learn how to make the day special for him. I tried very hard to make these days memorable and to give my boys something I never had ... a real Father's Day. They, in turn, were expected to be thinking of how they could make the day special for their dad by showing how much they loved him. The usual homemade cards would appear, along with any crafts or gifts we thought Jim would enjoy. I felt that my attempts to make Father's Day special improved every year. But this year, the phone rang shortly after our meal was finished. The boys and Jim had returned outside, and I was starting my usual chore of doing the dishes and cleaning up the kitchen. I checked the call display. I could tell it was a London number by the area code and then the first three numbers following that. For a brief moment, I considered letting the answering machine pick up. Then my detective instincts kicked in when I remembered my call a few days earlier to a London number.

I quickly reached for the receiver after the fourth ring, but it slipped through my fingers, falling towards the floor.

CHAPTER TWENTY-EIGHT

JUST A PHONE CALL AWAY

June 18, 2000 - Father's Day

I fumbled with the long, coiled phone cord and managed to pull the receiver towards my hand. I couldn't allow the receiver to hit the linoleum floor. After my lucky catch, I prayed the caller was still on the other end.

With sweaty palms and a racing heart, I managed to gasp, "Hello?" hoping I hadn't disconnected us.

The woman's voice on the other end was unfamiliar. I reached for my notes to check the number on the phone's call display against Joyce Hawkins' phone number. But before I had a chance to confirm, our conversation began.

"Hi. Is this Wendy Scott?" she asked.

"Yes, it is," I confirmed.

"Hi, Wendy. It's Joyce Hawkins. We spoke earlier this

week about you and your search. You have the right person." I dropped my notes and stood speechless.

I didn't quite understand what was happening. "I don't know what you mean by the right person. Could you explain please?"

"You have found your brother. His name is Darryl now. I had to see if it was okay with him before I confirmed it. I spoke with Darryl today and I now have his permission to tell you."

Joyce seemed quite excited to deliver this news and I was still in shock. She continued to tell me how she had verified my identity with the records they had been given when they had adopted Darryl in 1968. Their information stated that he had three sisters at the time, and this is why she had asked me about my siblings. Mine and my sisters' ages matched exactly to what was in her documents.

"So his name is Darryl Hawkins now. I just can't believe it. Joyce, I don't know if you realize this or not, but my maiden name was Hawkins. Do you think that is a coincidence or are you related somehow to my dad's family?" I asked.

"Oh my goodness, Wendy. That's a coincidence. I can hardly believe it!" Joyce answered. "I'll ask Ken if he knows anything about this, or if there is a possible connection between the two families. I highly doubt it, though, as I know all of Ken's family."

Joyce and I continued our conversation and I could

tell she was just as excited for this adventure as me. Apparently, I had first called her on Darryl's birthday, June 15, and they had just celebrated it today along with Father's Day. I hadn't given it any thought on Thursday when I called her. It was a pure coincidence, much like our last names both being Hawkins.

From the start, I liked Joyce. She had been very open and honest about the adoption, which was what the non-identifying information had stated. Darryl had been told from the start he had been adopted, and this was music to my ears. This made things a whole lot easier. I could tell from our early conversations, Joyce's friendly voice and kind personality would make her an excellent nurse and mother. She instantly became a person I could trust to share valuable information about Darryl's life. When she spoke of him, it was always very matter of fact; nothing was ever held back. Our conversation came so easily that I felt like I was chatting with a friend I had known all my life.

During my initial conversation with Joyce, I learned mostly basic information about Darryl. He was a tinsmith (sheet metal worker) and had a full-time permanent job. He had two boys from a previous relationship but was separated from their mother. They had not been married. The boys spent most of their time with their mom, but Darryl loved his kids to no end and was actively involved in their lives any chance he got. Learning that Darryl maintained a steady job and had two children and parents who loved him and his children gave me a huge sense of relief. By the way Joyce described him, I started to envision what his life was like, but still had no idea what he looked like. The non-identifying information described him as attractive, tall, blonde haired, and with very blue eyes, a long heart-shaped face, and a fair complexion. I wondered if any of those traits stayed with him and if he looked similar to any of us girls. Wanda had blonde hair and all of us had fair complexions. Maybe there would be some family resemblance. I hoped to meet him and find out for myself very soon.

Joyce remarked how Darryl had been overwhelmed by all the excitement of the day and finding out about my call. Based on this revelation, I felt our conversation wasn't going to end with me getting his phone number. My thoughts turned to trying to set up a future telephone date with him at her house, but then Joyce added the missing piece. She gave me his phone number! She said he wanted me to call him. I couldn't believe my luck as I stared down at his phone number. After seven long years of searching, I had finally found my half-brother. The final stepping stone was just a phone call away.

The excitement I felt after hanging up was unfathomable. Never again have I felt such relief, joy, peace, fulfillment, and pride all in one precious moment. Having children came close, but this was different. I had put my heart and soul into the search and now it was finished.

What was left I guessed would be the easy part—at least I thought it would be easy for us to get to know each other. But by the year 2000, we had both lived for thirty years or more and experienced many of life's tumbles, twists, and turns. Some good, and others maybe not so good. We would both have to decide how much of our previous lives we wanted to share and if a relationship could be established. Since we hadn't grown up together, we wouldn't have a sibling bond like the one I had with my sisters. We loved each other unconditionally, forgave one another, and accepted each other's faults ... that's what family does. Maybe if Darryl and I tried, we could grow something resembling a friendship.

I took a few moments by myself to savour my incredible accomplishment. Once I returned to earth from cloud nine, I considered my next steps. Joyce had said Darryl was a bit overwhelmed by all the excitement, so I decided to postpone calling him until the next day. Instead, I decided to spread the good news to my family.

Jim could tell something was up when he found me grinning like a Cheshire cat. Jim and the kids were all very excited when I shared the good news, and the boys immediately asked if this meant he would be their uncle. I explained that I still needed to call Darryl and feel him out, so to speak. Then, judging by our conversations, we would decide as a family if we wanted to pursue the relationship any further. Having a family meant protecting them, so earlier Jim and I had discussed the impact of inviting a total stranger into our lives. We would ensure the safety of our children by getting to know as much as possible about Darryl before any real contact was made.

Next, even though it was getting late, I knew who I had to call. Without my Watson, I may never have found Darryl.

"Hi, Lynn. It's Wendy."

"Oh, hi Wendy. How are you?" he asked nonchalantly.

"Lynn, I apologize for calling you so late, but I have to tell you something." It was difficult not to just blurt it out, but I wanted to keep him in suspense a bit longer.

"Oh, that's okay. I'm up for a while yet. What is it you want to tell me? Does it have anything to do with the last couple ... Ummm ... Hawkins. I believe their name was Hawkins?" Lynn asked.

"Yes. It was him. I mean it was them. They were the couple who adopted my half-brother! His name is Darryl now. I just can't believe it, Lynn." It still seemed so surreal, even after saying it out loud again.

"Well, isn't that something. You found him." He sighed and then asked, "Wendy, did you ask if they could be related somehow to you?" He was thinking now.

"Yes, Lynn, I did. Joyce said it's unlikely but she's going to ask Ken about it," I answered.

"So have you contacted him yet?" Lynn questioned.

"No. Not yet. I just found out tonight that I had the

right people, so I need some time to think. Joyce gave me his number so I'll probably call tomorrow. I just wanted to let you know because without your help I may not have found him, Lynn." I was so grateful and wanted him to know.

"Wendy. You did all the work. You had the non-identifying information and the list of nurses. All I had to do was check out some names in the directories and match them up. I just happened to be going to London and could help you out." Lynn did not want to take any credit for his part in our find. Even when I offered to pay for gas and long-distance calls he declined once again.

"I can never thank you enough, Lynn. This is one of the most exciting times in my life and I want you to know I'll be forever grateful for what you did. We have never even really met, just talked on the phone."

"That doesn't matter to me, Wendy. Just knowing you have found him is enough."

Lynn was content to end our relationship, never to meet face to face or speak again. I, on the other hand, felt we should. Maybe one day.

Laying in bed that night, I thought about all the research, calls, money, time, and emotions leading up to that final moment. It had taken seven years to build my path of stepping stones and now I had reached the end. Most times, every stone I moved to and uncovered didn't reveal much. But each stone I had laid down before me gave me new hope.

The non-identifying information had been the most useful bit of knowledge during my search. Really, I found Darryl because of it. But the other avenues like Sarnia and London Parent Finders, International Reunion Services, library microfiche, newspaper ads, private investigators, and The Adoption Disclosure Registry each served a purpose and made me a much better detective. I learned how to keep striving for my end goal and thinking of how to build new leads from the old ones. Other people have had success with the above-mentioned avenues, but for me the non-identifying information was key.

There was one avenue I left out of the above list. Barrie Parent Finders did not help in my search for Darryl (as mentioned in Chapter Twenty-Five), but it did lead to another awesome piece of the puzzle. This is not the time to share that just yet, but I will in a later chapter. Stay tuned.

June 19, 2000

The next morning, I awoke with a new sense of freedom. My search was finished, but now I needed to plan out what I wanted to say to Darryl. The boys and Jim had left for school and work, leaving me time to focus solely on building a list of questions in my head while also completing my household chores. I think best while working.

Joyce had mentioned that Darryl worked days, so evenings would be the best to give him a call. Once I was done with my chores, I immediately switched to my old routine of jotting down notes, and before long I had a lengthy list of possible questions and information I may want to share. Our grandfather had been diabetic, so I felt that was a priority to discuss, along with what little information I could share about our dad. I knew very little about his birth mother, but I was willing to call her again if the need arose. She had been quite open to answering any questions I had even though she didn't want to meet Darryl. She felt it would bring back too many bad memories. We had discussed how I would call her when I found her biological son, so eventually I would keep my word and make that call.

The evening finally came. My excitement had grown as the day passed, but so did my anxiety. It wouldn't be as simple as picking up the phone and talking to an old friend or family member. I would be striking up a conversation with a total stranger I hoped to build a relationship with.

I focussed on the one thing we had in common, our father. At that point, Darryl knew nothing about his parents, but I did. He had been adopted, so all that information was confidential. I could be the one to tell him about his birth parents if he wanted to know. I felt I had earned the right to divulge this information after seven long years of searching.

Supper was finished, the boys were busy, so now was the time. Jim was relaxing in front of the TV after a hard day at work. I picked up the phone and started punching in Darryl's number, but then I lost my nerve and hung up.

Jim looked up from the TV and noticed me standing, staring at the phone. He knew I planned to call Darryl after supper. "Well, are you going to call him or what?"

PART THREE

AFTER THE SEARCH

CHAPTER TWENTY-NINE

MAKING A CONNECTION

June 19, 2000

The phone did not ring many times before a deep, husky, male voice answered. With my handy, dandy list beside me, I felt confident we would have plenty to talk about. And we did.

"Hello, Darryl?" I asked.

"Yes, speaking. Is this Wendy?" He had been waiting for my call.

"Yes, Darryl. It's Wendy. I'm so glad I've finally found you! You know who I am, right?"

"Yes, Mom told me. So how are you?" Darryl seemed quite friendly and thoughtful .

"I'm very good. Finding you has made me even better. I just can't believe it's really true," I paused and then added, "Darryl. I have been searching for seven years and now it's over. What did you think when your mom told you?" From the start, I wanted us to have open conversations.

"I was so happy. I went and told my friends and the guys at work. I'm grinning from ear to ear right now, you know?" he laughed. "I'm the happiest guy alive!"

"You must be elated. Does it feel a bit unreal too?" I was feeling this way so I felt he might also.

"Yes, it does. But talking to you now, I know it's real," he confessed.

We eased into a conversation about how we currently filled our days, including details about our children and relationships. I told him about my marriage to Jim, and our two boys, Darian and Jason. He shared about his previous relationship with his children's mother, and how it had not been a good match. It ended rather poorly and she had moved on to another relationship. He had been dating but hadn't found that special someone yet. The way he spoke of his boys, I knew he was proud of Alex and Nick.

Next, we moved on to a more serious conversation about our dad. I started by asking him what exactly he knew about his birth and adoption, and why he had not come looking for anyone.

"Darryl. I want to ask you something personal. Why didn't you ever look for your birth parents?" This was something I had wanted to ask and now felt comfortable enough to do so.

"To be honest, I never thought anyone wanted me," he solemnly replied. This was not something I could have ever imagined. I was dumbfounded by his answer and felt so sorry he had to endure this feeling his whole life. I had previously thought with him being a guy maybe he just didn't care and was content with his adoptive parents. Now that I knew the truth, it stung. My heart went out to him. If I began to feel comfortable enough in our friendship, I would eventually try to show and tell him how much I wanted him in my life. Right now, he was still a stranger. Maybe just the fact that I had spent so much time and effort to locate him would show Darryl how much I cared.

For The Adoption Disclosure Registry, and my letter left at the C.A.S. in London to be of any value, he had to be looking for family also. But this was not the case. If only he had registered or went to the C.A.S., then maybe we would have been matched up. But fate had decided otherwise. Our destiny had been made possible through the non-identifying information.I had thought it would be the last possible way we would have found each other. We spoke on the phone several times a week, after that initial call. Each conversation had left me feeling closer to Darryl, and I soon realized we would eventually meet in person. He informed me that he had a brother who was married with a child of his own. Darryl knew about Wanda and Linda, so I filled him in on their husbands, children, and careers. He seemed interested in their lives and loved the idea of being an uncle, seven more times over. I became more open during our conversations over the next few months and eventually shared where we were all located. For me, trust took a bit of time to develop because I was trying to protect myself and family from someone we knew little about.

Darryl and I eventually had the serious discussion about his birth parents. I honestly don't remember when this took place ... if it happened during our first telephone conversation or not. I do remember Darryl was bewildered to find out about the death of our father. Up to this point, he had no idea if his parents were still alive, so I approached this subject slowly by sharing the information and telling the story I knew so well.

I began with my father and mother separating, leaving Mom to take care of us three girls by herself. Shortly after the separation, Dad had met Darryl's mom, Nancy, and she got pregnant right away. She was only in her teens. They both were too immature to support a baby and a relationship. So, a month after the baby was born, Nancy gave up custody and placed him in the care of the C.A.S. She then went to live with friends of Dad and he must have continued living in their rented apartment or done some couch surfing.

One early morning, Dad had broken into the Roby's house, threatened Darryl's mom, wrestled with the armed homeowner, Mr. Roby, and the gun went off. Our father died of a fatal gunshot wound to the heart.

When Darryl heard this, he was taken aback. He hadn't realized the possibility of having a parent within his grasp and then having them swept away at that same moment. He would never have the opportunity to meet his dad, in this life anyway, and so I tried to empathize by explaining I also had gone through life without him. Dad had left us when I was around two years old and didn't have time for us afterwards. He was busy with Nancy, Darryl's mother. He died when I was four and was not replaced by anyone. So in essence, he had left all four of us fatherless. Luckily, Darryl had been adopted by a loving and caring family. A family unit that still remained intact. So in the end, he had the opportunity to have a father.

This prompted a discussion about the coincidence of our family name, Hawkins. He could have possibly had that surname on his original birth certificate if Nancy had chosen to name him after our biological father. Initially, I remembered Darryl questioning the connection, and he had me explain it to him a few times. Then, in typical Darryl style, he would say, "I think it's cool."

Eventually, we also plunged into the emotionally difficult subject of Nancy, his birth mother. I had known it would come up eventually so I just told him the truth.

"What about Mom?"

"That's a touchy subject. I spoke with your mom on the phone once. I've never met her in person, but she was more than willing to answer any questions I had." I had to be careful how I broached this subject as Nancy had indicated that she didn't want a relationship with "Dwayne" if I should find him.

"What kind of questions?" Darryl asked.

"Oh, I asked her about your name at birth, your birthdate, stuff like that. She remembered your name and birth month, but not the actual day. Darryl, she was there that night Dad died. It was not easy for her," I carefully interjected.

"That must have been awful for her," Darryl sympathized.

"Yes, it was such a tragic event. She shared how it had impacted her life that night and how she went screaming down the street in shock and terror. Apparently, she saw him collapse on the bed after being shot, and he died in front of her." I tried to imagine this young mother seeing this and knowing she had just lost the man she once loved and the father of her child forever.

"Wow. My mom went through a lot." Darryl was slowly processing all this information.

"Yes, she did, Darryl. Their relationship was not so good either and so it's left her with a bit of a sour taste in her mouth. What I'm trying to say is she wants nothing to do with that part of her life. She said it's just too painful." There. I had said it ... kind of.

"What exactly are you saying? She doesn't want to meet me?" Darryl questioned.

"Unfortunately, that's what she wants. I haven't contacted her yet about finding you, but when I do, I'll ask again. In our last conversation, she said it would be too painful to get to know you. And she's worried you would be like our dad." I was not certain what she meant by that, but I could imagine some concern over unwanted qualities being passed on. Being unfaithful to his partner could have been one of the downfalls she had been implying.

I gave Darryl some of the details I knew about his mom. She was married and had two adult sons. I'm not sure if I ever told him where she lived but did explain how Aunt Myrna, dad's sister, knew her. They had both lived in the same town for most of their lives. She had been inclined to share everything she knew about the situation with me. I also told Darryl that Aunt Myrna had wanted to adopt him, but just felt she couldn't manage it at the time. She already had two young children of her own to care for.

"That's good to know she wanted to, but just couldn't. I understand," Darryl stated sincerely.

"I plan to share that I've found you with your mom, and we'll see where it goes from there. I'm sure she will be as excited as I am." I was honestly hoping everyone would feel as I did. Willing to forget the past and move on to what was important ... Darryl. It was only fair for him to get to know his biological family. It wasn't his fault that his parents had conceived him out of wedlock and then a tragedy had resulted in him being placed in foster care until he was eventually adopted.

Darryl and I had long phone conversations every week. I used my landline, and since it wasn't a long-distance call, it didn't cost me a dime. Darryl, on the other hand, used a cell phone most times. During one of our conversations, he casually mentioned he had to pay for our calls. I had assumed that when I called him he wouldn't incur any charges, but when he called me there would be a charge. Thinking I had it all figured out, most times I tried to be the one calling. Cell phones back then did not come with the kinds of plans they have these days so Darryl ended up with a fairly large phone bill after the first month. After his revelation, we started cutting our conversations short to avoid these charges. Boy, did I feel stupid and wished he had told me earlier. I think he was just trying to be nice, but I was relieved when he shared this.

These phone conversations allowed us to share different aspects of our lives, all from the comfort of our own homes. It was a safe way of getting to know one another and freely ask questions. The topics we discussed varied from where we attended school, to boyfriends and girlfriends, and also our family medical history. I told him about Grandpa Hawkins having diabetes and how it was genetic. He was deceased at this point. He had passed when I was pregnant with Jason in 1996. Other than that, I had no other health concerns to share. His mother's medical history was unknown to me, so I really couldn't comment about that.

I had thought during all of our conversations he would eventually ask for his mother's name. He never once asked me, so I never shared it. The fact Darryl had lived in London all his life was very fortunate for my search since there was then no need to follow a trail of moves. We discussed our children's interests and he mentioned that if I came to London for one of Darian's hockey games he would love to come by and watch. I shared about my life growing up in Arkona and that I still lived in a small town. Living in a city had never been a desire for me and probably never would be

Bit by bit, we each revealed snippets of information about ourselves. As I grew more comfortable and trusting of Darryl, I eventually gave him the name of my town, Inwood. Further chats revealed he had spent many summer vacations as a child with his Grandma in Petrolia, a small town just fifteen minutes from Inwood.

The next obvious step for us was to meet in person. Mutually, we had agreed on getting to know one another first, and after two months we both felt it was time. No red flags were up or waving at either of us, so we arranged a meeting in two weeks at his mom and dad's house in London. He may have wanted his parents there for moral support on neutral ground just like I needed someone there too. Someone who had supported me throughout the search. But who would I ask?

CHAPTER THIRTY

THE HAWKINS HOUSE

September 2000

By now, my immediate family knew I had found my long-lost half-brother. They wanted to hear the whole story of how I found Darryl, and of course they were astonished to learn his last name was Hawkins. They were a bit leery about his past, like I was initially, and asked me to think carefully before sharing personal information or meeting him. I reassured them that I had been careful and wouldn't rush into anything—we were taking our time and getting to know and trust each other.

Linda and Wanda were his sisters too, so it only made sense to invite them to our first meeting. They had been so supportive during my search by encouraging me to keep looking, and they were available when I just needed a listening ear. I thought they would be as excited to meet

Darryl as I was … to finally get to know our long-lost sibling. Linda declined for personal reasons, but Wanda gladly accepted the invitation. Like me, she was curious about Darryl and wanted to meet him. I arranged the meeting on a weekend I had no shifts at St. Francis Advocates. Jim agreed not to accept any call-in shifts so he could tend to the boys. Since I had organized the meeting, it would be my responsibility to get us there. Wanda and I would rendezvous close to the 402 (a large highway in our area) and carpool from there. We would leave just after lunch so we didn't interrupt anyone's meals.

The fall day was perfect driving weather. The sun was shining through the windshield, warming my face as I concentrated on the road ahead. Temperatures were seasonal and I felt comfy in pants and a short-sleeved shirt. Alone in my car, I wondered if this was the right thing to do. I was feeling a bit nervous and anxious and I allowed negative thoughts to surface. I then reminded myself of the struggle it took to get to this point and how God would not allow all this to happen if it wasn't for something good. I then prayed my usual prayer for safe travels, to watch over my family and friends, and finally asked for strength and guidance at the meeting.

I picked Wanda up and could tell she was eager to meet Darryl. She had a nervous, mischievous smile, almost as if to say, "Are you ready for this, Wendy?" Her large green eyes were dancing with excitement. I knew only too well this meant we were in for an adventure.

When any of us girls got together, there was hardly ever a quiet moment. We would always have lots to talk about and enjoyed catching up on each other's lives. It was at that particular point I knew that whatever happened in my life I would always have Wanda. She had my back and we would navigate anything together.

The one hour drive from the rendezvous point to London flew by as we chatted. We discussed how nervous we were and who would do most of the talking. We decided it would be a joint venture, with both of us asking questions as the meeting progressed.

We pulled up in the driveway and looked around. Darryl's parents lived in a fairly modest home situated in a pleasant neighbourhood. It was the type of practical home where kids would feel welcome and relaxed. Joyce, Darryl's mom, welcomed us into her home and we introduced ourselves. She escorted us into the living room where we met Darryl. He appeared to be very happy, but shy, about meeting us. He wouldn't really look us in the eye, and every once in a while when our eyes would meet, he would quickly look down again.

I found Darryl to be quite a handsome man, of average height, with a slim build, blondish brown hair, and an eye colour I couldn't quite pinpoint. They looked gray at times, but it was hard to get a good look since our eye contact was minimal.

We sat down together in the living room and Joyce began filling us in on Darryl's childhood. She found it difficult to bond with him as a baby and wondered if it was because he was given up for adoption as an infant. Early on in his childhood, Darryl was diagnosed with ADHD (Attention Deficit Hyperactivity Disorder). Joyce, having a nursing background, used her extensive knowledge to ensure he received proper treatment, dietary nutrition, and medication for his diagnosis.

Based on his history, I thought Darryl must have been a very complex child, and later quite a challenging teenager. As an adult, though, he seemed very bright and I noticed he had extensive knowledge about cars and music—-two of his favourite subjects. He explained how his love of listening to very loud music in his younger years had contributed to his partial hearing loss. He had attended many concerts and loved sitting next to the gigantic speakers.

Due to his good looks, Darryl said he had many relationships with women. He openly admitted he loved women, shopping (because that's what women like), and dating. It was rather unfortunate that his relationship with Alex and Nick's mother hadn't worked out. Years after I found Darryl, she passed away. I never had the opportunity to meet her. Darryl maintained steady employment as a tinsmith. This type of work, he explained, was hard on the hands and used mathematical skills to fabricate ductwork for heating and ventilating systems. He also offered to make me a dustpan if I ever wanted one. I should have taken him up on it. I bet it would have lasted a lifetime!

Joyce, like she had been on the phone, was extremely easy to talk with. Ken, her husband, had confirmed they were in no way related to our Hawkins family. My finding Darryl, plus him having the same last name, had truly been a "one in a million" chance. Joyce excused herself at that point, allowing time for us three to chat alone.

Wanda opened the conversation, commenting about the physical resemblances between us all and the more prominent ones like his and our dad's cleft chin. Wanda, being two years older than me, had vivid memories of our dad so I always looked to her for information about him.

After chatting for about half an hour, we went to meet his dad and children. His dad, Ken, was friendly enough and his boys, Alex and Nick, were sweet. They were around my boys' ages so the conversations revolved around their similar interests, video gaming being the most popular one. Darryl's mom had taken them under her wing and made sure they were involved in lots of activities, including attending church when they stayed at her and Ken's house. We ended our visit outside, getting some great photos in the laneway. Darryl was quite exuberant in all of them and probably climbing that ladder, in his head, to cloud nine. Our hugs goodbye seemed a bit awkward but were necessary for our relationship to grow. It was just one of those moments where you knew it had been a long time coming so it seemed appropriate.

With time, those hugs would become more natural and help us form a sibling bond. On the way home, Wanda and I talked about how comfortable it felt to be with Darryl. We both agreed that he could pass for our brother ... even his hands were similar to ours. Wanda remembered Dad's stature and said Darryl's was a close comparison. We did wonder about the lack of eye contact and found this to be a bit odd. But we reminded ourselves he was pretty shy and that it would likely improve over time. "Something to work on," I thought.

The day I met Darryl. Left to right - Me, Darryl, and Wanda

To say I felt good that day would be an understatement. It felt utterly phenomenal to finally meet the brother I had been searching for. It was a bonus to find out he had been adopted by a wonderful family and had two healthy, adorable boys. Closure wrapped its wide-open arms tight.

The last few months of the year were filled with updating friends and family on how the meeting with Darryl went. Everyone was so pleased to hear it had gone well. Darryl and I maintained phone contact, but as I mentioned earlier we kept our calls short to reduce the cost to him. Plus we scheduled visits when I was going to be in or near London for hockey with the boys. Pizza Hut was our favourite go-to restaurant, as the boys loved stuffed cheese crust pizza and Darryl just loved to eat.

Aunt Myrna wanted to hear all about Darryl, so I set up a visit for the two of us. She listened intently as I explained every detail of the meeting and described his appearance and good upbringing by Ken and Joyce Hawkins. Their confirmation of having no blood relation to our Hawkins family was substantiated by Aunt Myrna. She too felt there was no connection, just a coincidence of having the same name. Darryl's boys were a soft spot for her as she loves children and wanted to hear all about them. By her tears of joy, I could tell she was happy to hear all about his good upbringing and family life. It helped alleviate any guilt she felt for not adopting him. She asked if I had called Nancy yet, but I told her no ... soon though.

During the visit, she gave me some of my dad's personal items. The wallet contained his driver's licence, birth certificate, Department of Labour registration card, Canadian Red Cross blood identification card,

Social Insurance Number card, and a picture of him and Nancy. The photo had been taken at one of those old photo booths and it showed them happy and smiling. One of their scarce good times, I guess. They both looked so young.

Aunt Myrna also had a rare picture of Nancy and baby Dwayne. She had held onto it for years. It must have been taken during a visit to the C.A.S. shortly after Nancy gave him up for adoption. Dwayne looks around three months old. I had thought it would be something Aunt Myrna wouldn't want to part with, but she did.

Lastly, she gave me all of dad's funeral keepsakes, including the guest book. That was where I found my name written down, along with Miss Barber, Dorothy, and Jean. But it was not the handwriting of a four-year-old child. One of them had signed it for me. It was interesting to see the names of people I knew in that book and thought about how they must have been so horrified by the tragic event.

During the writing of this book, I found out that Mom had stayed a week with Grandpa and Grandma Hawkins after my dad's death. That would explain why I went home with the three ladies after the funeral. Mom also revealed that dad was still wearing his wedding ring when he was killed. To me, this could either mean he still felt married to Mom and didn't feel right taking it off, or he was pretending to be married to Nancy. I will never know.

I finally felt ready to call Nancy. Talking with Aunt Myrna had spurred me on. She seemed to think Nancy would want to know about Darryl. My gut instinct had been to wait until after I met Darryl and could give her positive information about his life. Now, after meeting him, I knew my report would be worthy of her scrutiny. Given the admirable upbringing by the Hawkins family and Darryl's industrious and upbeat personality, maybe she would have second thoughts.

Seven years had passed since I last spoke to Nancy. She had been adamant about not wanting to meet Dwayne. I was hoping she hadn't changed her phone number or moved. My accumulation of papers, handwritten notes, documents, newspaper clippings, and letters from agencies were all kept in a brown manilla envelope. It had been completely stuffed full, and contained every bit of information I had ever received or sent regarding Darryl. As I went in search of her number in the envelope, visions of a mother and son reunion flooded my mind.

I remembered how Aunt Myrna had handed me Nancy's name and phone number on a pale yellow sticky note. After emptying the envelope onto the kitchen table, I quickly scanned the contents and waited for something yellow to catch my eye. When I didn't see anything, I carefully scrutinized each piece of paper, front and back, thinking it may have got stuck somewhere. Nothing.

Out of frustration I called the boys in from playing outside ready to interrogate them. I wondered if they had been messing around and accidentally knocked the envelope and its belongings out onto the floor. That sticky note would have been long gone.

As I heard the boys racing inside the back door, it suddenly dawned on me there was one place I hadn't checked.

CHAPTER THIRTY-ONE

NEVER A DAY GOES BY

November 2000

I had forgotten to check the **inside** of the envelope. Since it was a sticky note, the possibility of it still being in the envelope was highly possible. I peered into the envelope, and carefully pulled it off the side.

"Never mind boys," I said as they came bounding in, "I found it." Being the casual, carefree boys that they were, and wanting to get back outside, they quickly spun around and headed back out. They didn't even ask what I had wanted. Somehow, I knew my journey would not end when I found Darryl; it would only be the beginning. Deep down I knew I would try to unite "baby Dwayne" with his mom Nancy. Nancy had surrendered him to the C.A.S. thirty-three years ago. Since then, Darryl had grown up into a good man. Maybe Nancy could be ready to meet him once she discovered he had been found.

The phone rang and a male voice answered. I asked if I could speak to Nancy and luckily she was there. They hadn't moved after all. I sent up a little prayer, thanking God for this small miracle. No need to put my detective skills to the test again. "Hello?" a female voice on the other end said.

"Hi, Nancy. It's Wendy Scott calling. I'm Leonard Hawkins' daughter." I asked it with a hint of questioning in my voice to see if she would remember me.

"Who is this? I don't understand who you are," she asked.

This wasn't going to be as easy as I had imagined. I wasn't sure if she was playing stupid or actually didn't remember me.

"It's Wendy Scott, Nancy. I'm Leonard Hawkins' daughter. We spoke on the phone quite a few years ago about the baby you put up for adoption." There. I had stated it and now something should jog her memory.

"Are you saying you are my daughter?" she questioned.

"No. I'm Leonard's daughter, Wendy. Remember how I questioned you about giving Dwayne up for adoption before my father was killed? You also knew my stillborn baby was buried on top of my dad because you visited his grave." By now, I was feeling a little confused as to whether that telephone conversation had ever happened.

"Okay. Sorry. It's just been so long and I wasn't sure who you were. Now I understand." Finally, we were getting somewhere.

"Nancy, the reason I'm calling is that I have some

wonderful news. I've found Dwayne!" Silence. The silence went on for too long, so I added, "I met him recently and he lives in London. Not that far away from where you live."

"Oh. What's he like?" she asked.

"Well, he's very handsome. He doesn't have the black hair like my dad, but probably it's more like yours ... blondish-brown. He's a kind man and was raised by a good family in London. I met them also along with his two boys. He has children so you are their grandmother." I threw that in, hoping to appeal to her heart.

"What's his mom like?" she asked.

"Very kind and caring. She's a nurse. Nancy, they did a good job raising him." I replied.

"Does he work?" she asked next.

"Yes. He apprenticed, went to college, and now works full time as a tinsmith. He's a sheet metal worker. He said it's hard on his hands, causing lots of cuts." I wanted to show her how well he was doing, so I also added that he had held his current job for a very long time. He was a hard worker.

"I'm glad he had a good family and is doing well. Never a day goes by that I don't think about him," she softly said.

I revealed that Dwayne's name was now Darryl Hawkins. She was astounded at the possibility of him having that last name and could barely believe it.

Nancy shared that her boys knew nothing about Darryl's existence, only her husband knew. That was the main reason why she didn't want to meet him. Also, she mentioned that she was worried about the painful memories a reunion might surface. She thought he would be just like my dad and she couldn't cope with that.

"Are you sure, Nancy? I could be there to introduce you. You'd have the chance to meet your grandchildren too." I begged her to change her mind, but she wouldn't budge.

"It would just be too painful," she confessed.

"If you change your mind, please call me. Just to let you know, he's never asked me for your name so we'll leave it at that. Based on our last conversation, I kept your name anonymous. If he does ask me, which I don't think he will, I won't lie, Nancy."

With my personality type, I find it hard to lie when asked a question on the spot. That is not to say I haven't lied before, but I find it difficult to live with. I usually end up telling myself to make it right and this lessens my guilty conscience. Darryl had the right to know his mom's name, so if he asked, I would tell him.

I left my name and phone number, just in case Nancy changed her mind or wanted to talk more about Darryl. She never did call me, but this doesn't mean she no longer plays a role in my path forward. A stepping stone would eventually appear out of nowhere when I least expected it, one that I didn't have to search for. Another ghost from Nancy's past.

May 22, 2001

I am not sure what took me so long, but I finally called

the C.A.S. to announce my incredible news about finding Darryl. It had been almost a year since my discovery, and it was past time to thank my caseworker for all her help.

Sometimes when you are expecting more to happen than what does, you are left feeling disappointed. This was the case when I called her. Maybe I wanted her to ask for all the details of my search, what Darryl was like, or just how things were going with us in general. I suppose she did her job according to the expected duties, but I wanted more. I wanted to hear and feel elation in her voice. If it wasn't for the non-identifying information, which the C.A.S. had provided, I never would have found him. I told her this but didn't get the response I expected.

She calmly said she was glad for me, and if Darryl wanted any information, he was able to contact her. That was it. Done. Talk about bittersweet. Maybe she was happy I wouldn't be endlessly calling for updates anymore. In some odd way, I was going to miss the search ... the adventure of it all.

CHAPTER THIRTY-TWO

NEW BEGINNINGS AND REUNIONS

June 2001

Our little family deserved more social and economic opportunities than Inwood could provide. Plus the boys needed more room to roam. So after a lot of discussion we decided that after sixteen years in Inwood it was time for a change. Sambo, our faithful tomcat, had passed away the previous winter, and his death just added to the list of reasons to move. He had become very ill in the fall, and after letting him out, I had a feeling it wasn't a good idea. I knew he loved us and would want us to take care of him always, even when he was ill. That is why it surprised me when he never returned. It was then I realized that animals do go away to die. We found him months later in our neighbour's shed.

Jim scouted out possible areas for us to live and found a property in a very upscale neighbourhood along the St. Clair River near Mooretown, Ontario. The home was closer to Jim's job and still within a reasonable drive to both of our families. The boys both could remain in French Immersion at a school in the neighbouring town of Corunna. It would be a farther drive for Darryl but one worthy of the extra miles.

The home had been built after the Second World War, along a picturesque county road called St. Clair Parkway. We would be the home's second owner. A few other wartime homes were close by, but the surrounding properties were being quickly bought up, torn down, and the property used to build gigantic modern homes. We used to joke that the neighbouring mansion had a brick wall probably worth the same as our entire house. We took possession of our new home before our actual move in July so we could do some much-needed renovations. We planned on restoring the original hardwood floors and freshening up the walls with some new paint. Most weekends were spent at the new home, and weekdays in Inwood, until the boys finished school.

The bungalow was situated on a little over an acre, so plenty of land for the boys to ride dirt bikes and three-wheelers. They could easily ride alongside the railroad tracks at the back of the property and access another trail at the end, leading in behind the tracks. Initially, these nearby tracks and the adjacent river had caused me some concern for my youngest, Jason. Before moving, I was envisioning him either drowning or being run over by a train. These concerns dissipated quickly after we moved in and became comfortable with our surroundings. The neighbours to the north of us had two boys with all the motorized toys and similar interests to our boys. Soon close friendships grew easily for the four of them. Now they all had even more room to ride as both yards were joined together with no fencing in between.

Looking west from our front bay window, we could see the beautiful St. Clair River. When the trees across the road were bare during winter and early spring, we had a spectacular view. For the longest time, Jim and I thought the property directly across the road had no house built on it. From our perspective, it looked like an empty lot. One winter day, though, we noticed smoke rising from somewhere across the road and wondered if we were imagining it.

On Christmas Day, another neighbour from across the road visited us. He introduced himself as Gord and offered the hill in his backyard to the boys to use for sledding. The only rule would be for an adult to accompany them. When our family ventured over, we discovered all the houses over there had a huge steep hill behind them, with the river at the bottom. Gord also offered his dock for fishing and his beach for swimming. The property directly across from us had enough room for a house at the bottom of its hill, with the river beyond that. The smoke we had seen must have been coming from their chimney. Were we ever surprised to discover this after six months of living there.

My job at St. Francis Advocates started with a few shifts per month and then gradually increased to way more than I had first agreed to. Since they wouldn't cut back on my hours I applied for the same type of work at a place in Sarnia. The new organization was called Christian Horizons and was similar to St. Francis in that they provided homes for people with disabilities. The main difference being it was faith-based. My Christian background and time in the Pentecostal Church afforded me the pleasure of working in this rewarding position. Like the other position was initially, I was mainly a casual employee with a few scheduled shifts each month. Darryl commended me on the type of work I did helping others and said it really wasn't something he could ever do. He was the sort of guy who enjoyed working in his shop by himself.

My flexible schedule enabled me time to volunteer at the boy's school in Corunna where I helped with reading programs. I valued the time spent with each child and loved watching them become more confident every week when we read together. I was also available to go on class field trips if Jason and Darian "allowed me" to volunteer.

Jim helped out on field trips when he had time off from his job as a high-pressure water operator. He had worked for a few companies since we first met doing the same type of work. The companies offered environmental high-pressure water work to chemical plants in Sarnia. It was dangerous work and Jim had to be safety conscious at all times or he could seriously injure himself with the lance. The pressure was strong enough to cut metal, rubber, cement, and human limbs. His job involved a lot of shift work, making it difficult to plan anything. Most days, we just had to go with the flow. In comparison, Darryl's jobs had always been during regular work hours with only the occasional overtime Saturday shift. He found the demands of Jim's job hard to comprehend and often questioned how Jim balanced his work and family life.

I would switch organizations and job titles three more times before settling into my current career as an E.A. (Educational Assistant) with the Lambton Kent District School Board. It took me longer than most people to become a full-time permanent E.A., as I didn't have the opportunity to attend college for that career. Instead, I leveraged job experiences to get to my current position. It may have taken longer, but I appreciate all the valuable skills I learned and the people I met along the way.

Darryl and I discussed our different education opportunities and he applauded my perseverance and ability to achieve my goals the hard way. Since Darryl's parents had earned a modest income, he told me that going to college or university had never been an option. It wasn't due to a lack of ambition or intelligence. He was very bright and a quick study. He said that he had difficulty staying on the right track and focusing on the future, otherwise he would have furthered his career into something with a much higher income.

2001-2005

Life gradually moved along and we started to settle down in our new home and lives. Darryl would occasionally drive down for the day and was especially proud to show off his red Mustang. He commented that we were very lucky to have such a beautiful view of the St. Clair River and such a lovely home and expansive yard. He would often say that he felt so relaxed coming to our home and getting away from the city. Our relationship started growing stronger and feeling more comfortable. The hugs no longer felt awkward when we said our hellos and goodbyes. Things were headed in the right direction ...

A year after finding Darryl, I invited him to a Hawkins family reunion. They had always been held at a conservation area in Cambridge, Ontario. All of Grandpa and Grandma Hawkins's side of the family were invited so potentially there could be up to a hundred people in attendance. The trip was about a two-hour drive for me and a one-hour drive for Darryl.

Darryl brought his two boys, Alex and Nick, so our boys could get better acquainted in the fun family setting. The boys all played together quite well and got involved with the games and activities planned by the family in charge that year.

This was the perfect opportunity to introduce my dad's side of the family to Darryl. I had been certain they all would have heard of his "arrival" by now. I had hoped they knew the tale of his conception and adoption so I would be spared telling those details. If anyone had asked questions, I had been prepared to tell them we would discuss it one-on-one at a later date. Thankfully no one went there.

I had been so passionate in my search for Darryl you would think I would be elated to introduce him to everyone. At times, though, I felt some trepidation as to whether people would be wondering why he was there. It was me who had found him and invited him, and I worried people would judge me for that. He was born out of wedlock after all, and some people feel things like that are better off left alone. No doubt it was just my usual negative thoughts creeping in, and I didn't let them stop me. At long last, Aunt Myrna met Darryl. She was the aunt who had wanted to adopt baby Dwayne but just couldn't make it work. This was the highlight of my day, to watch her readily accept Darryl as part of our family and then be completely engrossed in conversation with him for most of the day. She was beaming the whole time and Darryl was too. She continued to stay in contact with him via Facebook, evidence they had made a good connection. Grandma Hawkins and other family members met Darryl and his boys, and my sister Linda and her family did as well.

I believe it was the following year that another one of my dad's sisters met Darryl at the annual reunion. Auntie Fay wrote me a brief email afterwards explaining how she and her husband had also contemplated adopting baby Dwayne. She said, "In which case, I would now be his Mom." She stated how there was a strong family resemblance and Darryl had many of his dad's traits, even his voice reminded her of him. This sent shivers down my spine as I had often wondered if his raspy voice and good looks were compliments of my dad. Now I know.

Also in that email, Auntie Fay included some family history for me to share with Darryl. Our Grandpa Hawkins's grandparents came from Ireland and then settled in the United States. They had many children, one of whom was named Leonard (same as my dad) J. Hawkins who went up to Canada. He settled in Biggar, Saskatchewan and also had many children, and one was Grandpa Hawkins.

Grandma Hawkins's parents (nee Watson) came from England to Canada before she was born. They too settled near Biggar, Saskatchewan and stayed there all their lives. I guess the rest is history as to how my Grandpa and Grandma met. Maybe I should ask her someday. At the time of writing this, she is 103 years old and still lives on her own. What a lady!

So, I had two aunts who would have adopted Darryl

if their circumstances had allowed it. It was so enlightening to know how much they had cared about him, and I really appreciated them sharing this with me. I never would have thought this revelation would impact me but it did. I felt much closer to both of my aunts after learning about this. Being that we only visited the Hawkins family during the holidays, as a child I had never really gotten to know my aunts that well. I have since felt much more involved and a part of my dad's family. My sisters and our families all try to attend as many Hawkins events as possible and feel very loved and welcomed.

Labour Day long weekends while living on St. Clair Parkway found us camping in our expansive backyard. We invited people from both Jim's family and mine. Our yard, being over an acre, made a pretty good little campground for tents, trailers, bonfires, picnic tables, lawn chairs, three-wheelers, dirt bikes, and go-karts. Darryl and his boys, along with my two sisters and their families, enjoyed a few campouts and getting to know our new " little brother." We loved teasing him about this and he sucked it all in, meaning he loved it! Having three older sisters was as new to him as having a younger brother was for us.

Jim was the campfire expert and enjoyed cooking everything on an open fire. Not surprising given how much he loved barbequing. His tender, slow-roasted meats were always a hit, the longer they roasted the better. All weekend he would have that fire going, just like when we were camping during our summer holidays. His favourite meal to cook over the fire was bacon and eggs for breakfast. He would even do the toast on the grill. My job was prep and cleanup as I never really liked getting all that smoke in my eyes and hair. It was too much like BBQing for this woman!

In addition to our well-stocked food supply for the campout, most guests would contribute a fair amount. Our crew, consisting of mainly boys (only one girl), was always well fuelled for their fun-filled days of non-stop action. Chips, pop, hamburgers and spider dogs (weiners cut so when roasted over the fire they formed legs) were our camping food go-tos. Roasted, gooey marshmallows atop chocolate-covered digestive cookies topped off the night-time campfire for a nice sugary S'more treat. Mmmmmm.

Sometimes it was so cold in the evenings that we had sat huddled under blankets around the fire, and felt the dew settling on top of the fabric covering us. Gazing at the vast, dark night sky and being in awe of all the stars brought a sense of peace and calm after a busy day. It was a perfect time to reflect on the most memorable events of the day.

On a typical weekend such as this, most guests camped out for one night. We set up our tent trailer for Darryl and his boys to sleep in, and my sisters and their families slept in tents they positioned in the backyard. The kids would ride around on their motorized toys, while the adults sat and chatted around the campfire. Gord had offered his beach for swimming, so some of us would head over to cool off during the heat of the afternoon. Since the kids were always the focal point we packed these weekends full of fun, family-oriented activities.

These weekends were especially busy for Jim and me. Being the hosts meant entertaining, cooking, and making sure everyone was happy. It was so worth our efforts as everything always went quite smoothly. We thought these moments would never end and were hoping the memories would be forever etched in our children's minds.

August 2005

It happened just before Labour Day weekend in 2005. Ontario summers can be very hot and humid, some might even call them unbearable. Escaping to air conditioning or the shade of a tall, leafy tree can be your only means of coping with the heat. Fortunately for us, we lived close to the St. Clair River and Lake Huron so we frequently visited their beaches to cool off. We also had an above ground swimming pool in the backyard, if we just felt like staying home.

August is typically a hot month, and this year was no exception. Thankfully though, the nights were beginning to cool off so you could sit outside after supper for a while, at least until the mosquitoes came and carried you away. That usually happened shortly after dusk, and since it starts to get darker earlier, the timeframe to relish that coolness seemed to recede steadily. We also knew that when the days got shorter, this signalled that summer was almost over.

The boys had been splashing away in the pool, while Jim and I settled down in our lawn chairs, discussing plans for the next day. I had brought the cordless phone outside and set it on the patio table just in case someone needed to contact us. The phone rang and we both stared at it, hoping it wasn't work calling one of us at the last minute. I didn't recognize the number, as it was out of our area, but I decided to pick it up even though it was probably a telemarketer. I was in one of those moods to "play around with them" and had a few ideas of some great comebacks should they try to sell me something. I never had the opportunity to put my repertoire to the test. "Hello. Is this Wendy Scott?" a female voice asked.

"Yes, it is," I answered excitedly, ready for some fun.

"Hi. This is Donna. Do you remember registering with Barrie Parent Finders?"

I certainly was not expecting that to come out of her mouth. This was not a telemarketer, and I was very intrigued.

"Who did you say this was again?" I asked. At this point, I was thinking she was from Barrie Parent Finders. I was ready to tell her that I had found Darryl and wouldn't need my name registered with their organization anymore.

"My name is Donna. You don't know me, but I'm calling because I think you are my sister."

She had my attention.

CHAPTER THIRTY-THREE

ANOTHER BIG FIND

In Chapter Twenty-Five, I mentioned how sometimes in life you do things and unknowingly they lead to something else. When I registered with Barrie Parent Finders it didn't help me find Darryl. But what had seemed useless at the time really changed my life in ways I couldn't even imagine.

August 2005

Donna's statement left me dumbfounded. I sat frozen like a statue with the phone to my ear while my mind raced. I considered hanging up. Her suggestion was utterly preposterous. There was no way she could be my sister. But then I recalled Dad's indiscretion with Nancy. And I remembered Mom telling us way back when we were children that she wouldn't be surprised if we had other half-siblings besides the one she knew about between Dad and Nancy.

I proceeded with caution.

"Yes, I did register with them, but what makes you think I'm your sister?" I asked carefully but kindly.

"I also registered with Barrie Parent Finders and recently received a phone call from them saying they found a match between our registrations," she informed me.

"Okay. I still don't understand how we could be sisters. What was the match?" My interest was piqued and I was trying to make sense of it all.

"I registered with Barrie Parent Finders as an adoptee. I'm looking for my birth parents along with my half-brother who was born in 1967 in London. He was put up for adoption, much like myself, at an early age. It's my understanding you are looking for your half-brother, Dwayne Michael Gunness, who was born in 1967 and put up for adoption," she stated.

"Yes. All that is true, Donna, but I still don't understand the connection," I interjected.

"The match they found between us is the last name Gunness. At birth, I was named Heather Rose Gunness. So, now do you see the connection? Dwayne and I could be brother and sister," she said matter of factly.

It was all suddenly becoming clearer. Nancy had given up one baby for adoption and could very easily have had another and given it up too. Her maiden name was Gunness and if Dwayne was named that at birth then most certainly history could have repeated itself with Donna.

"When was your birthday, Donna?" I asked.

"I was born in London on October 21, 1968. According to the information you entered into the Barrie Parent Finders database that would be about 16 months after Dwayne was born. His birthday is June 15, 1967, right?"

That would have given Nancy enough time to get pregnant again and have another baby if there were sixteen months in between. Now I was indeed believing the possibility of Donna's story.

"Yes, Donna, that's his birthday. I feel there is a strong connection here and with so many facts lining up it must be true. If it is, though, you understand we aren't really sisters?" I hesitantly said.

"Oh yes, I get it. I was just thinking that if we share the same brother, it kind of makes us sisters, in a sense," she said jokingly.

"Okay. I get where you are coming from now. For a minute there, I thought my dad had somehow had another child until you told me your birth date. He died long before that, making it impossible for you to be his."

"So it sounds like Dwayne and I share the same mother. Every time she got pregnant at a young age and didn't know what to do she gave us up for adoption." Donna seemed certain she had reached the right person and I was thinking the same. It all seemed to match up.

"Donna, this is all such a shock but I believe you. I did find Dwayne some years back and have been in touch with him ever since. I also know your mother's name and have her contact information. " I said.

"You even know my mother's name? Wow. I can't believe this. Nothing like killing two birds with one stone!" Donna laughed.

"I know, right? You hit it big when you got in touch with me. When I registered with Barrie Parent Finders, never did I think it would lead to something other than finding Dwayne," I responded.

"So where do we go from here?" Donna asked.

"I'm going to think this through tonight and I'll get back to you tomorrow, Donna. Can I have your number?" I asked.

"Of course. Absolutely. I understand, Wendy, why you need some time to absorb all this."

Donna left me her contact information, and when I got off the phone I was unsure as to my next move. I wondered how on earth it could be proven that what she was saying was true. It was possible Nancy had another baby in that timeframe, but I wondered if someone would have really done that ... given up two babies for adoption.

When common sense failed me, I prayed to the one who could make all things clear. I prayed for the wisdom to know what to do as people's emotions were at stake. Never did I imagine that finding Darryl would impact so many people. I went to bed unsure what to do next.

By morning, God had provided me with the perfect

solution—call Aunt Myrna. She had long been my go-to for accurate information, and so far had been very forthcoming in sharing whatever she remembered about the past. Later that day when I called, I was happy to find Aunt Myrna was home. After the usual pleasantries, I warned her I had an odd question. Then I proceeded to ask if Nancy had happened to get pregnant again and give the baby up for adoption too? "Yes," she said. I couldn't believe it. "Wendy, Nancy did have another baby who she gave up. And I have a pretty good idea who the father was." But she didn't share his name with me and I didn't ask. I then told her the story about how I had registered with Barrie Parent Finders while looking for Darryl and how a person called Donna was claiming to be his half-sister. Now that she had backed up Donna's story, any doubts I had were gone. Donna was Nancy's daughter and Darryl had family he didn't even know about. I thanked Aunt Myrna for her help and promised to keep her updated.

The next person I needed to contact was Darryl. He would be shocked by this news, so I knew I would have to gradually ease into it. But I was also very eager to let him know he had a half-sister and hoped he could build a connection with her like he had with me.

I called Darryl right away and explained how Donna had found me through Barrie Parent Finders, and I recounted the story Aunt Myrna had told me. Before long, he was convinced. We agreed that Donna would not bother contacting me if it wasn't true. He had said it was okay to share his information and phone number with Donna. And I gave him Donna's number too in case he wanted to contact her first.

Once again, Darryl had a stranger searching for him to tell him they were family. Now this doesn't happen too often and I was a bit worried how he would cope. But knowing Darryl as I did, I imagined he would love having another biological sibling.

Time to call Donna with the good news.

"Hi, Donna. It's Wendy Scott. How are you doing?" I asked.

"Oh, hi Wendy. I'm doing well but was getting anxious waiting to hear back from you," she excitedly exclaimed.

"Well, I have an answer for you that you are going to like. You are indeed related to my half-brother and I can tell you all about him—in fact, he's excited to talk to you. And I also have information about your mother." I offered.

"You're kidding me, right?" she questioned.

"No. Not kidding, so here it goes. Your mother's name is Nancy Gunness and your brother's name now is Darryl Hawkins. Darryl has never asked me for your mother's name so he doesn't know this information. You can feel free to tell him, but I have always felt that if he wanted to know, he'd ask me."

For the next hour, I shared everything I knew about Nancy and Darryl's lives. Donna was extremely interested in knowing she had two more half-brother's, Nancy's boys, and was an aunt to Darryl's children. She shared how she was married and had a boy approximately the same age as my son Jason and Darryl's son Nick. Donna mentioned her military background and that she had been in the process of obtaining her pilot's license, which was an added benefit for her work as a private investigator. She presented herself as being quite a respectable person and I admired her spunk and career ambitions. During our conversation, I wrestled with sharing Nancy's phone number without her consent. I weighed Nancy's right for privacy and anonymity against Donna's right for full disclosure and closure. I struggled with my decision as I knew it could change lives, but who was I to say if it would lead to a negative or positive outcome.

Donna's need for closure reminded me of how I felt during my long search for Darryl, so I decided to give her both Darryl and Nancy's contact information. I had hoped Nancy would be open to communicating with Donna and would share lots of family history with her. Darryl could benefit from it as well.

What joy and relief I felt after our phone conversation. If Nancy was Donna's mother and Darryl was Donna's half-brother it would be such a life-changing event for all of them. "Maybe Nancy will feel the same way,"

I thought. But based on our previous conversations, I wouldn't bet on a reunion anytime soon.

Darryl and Donna connected later that week. I don't remember who reached out first, but I eventually got to hear about both versions of the telephone conversation. They decided to meet and asked me to arrange and mediate their introduction.

By this point, I had been working for the public school board for one year in a role I loved dearly and fortunately had summers off. I would soon be returning to work at Wallaceburg District Secondary School in the Developmentally Delayed/Medically Fragile Classroom, now known as the Alternative Learning and Life Skills Program, after Labour Day. The boys would also be returning to school and starting hockey once again, along with power skating. Given how busy things would get soon, I knew I had better set up Darryl and Donna's introduction sooner rather than later.

As I looked at my calendar, I scanned the available dates left in August but every weekend was full. I sighed and flipped the calendar to September and found the first available day for the introduction. Sunday, September 18 seemed like the only day that could work, so I called Donna and Darryl to confirm that date and select a time and location. I felt blessed and honoured to arrange the meeting.

There was just one more person I wanted to contact about attending the little get-together. She even lived in the city where we planned to meet. I was certain she didn't expect to hear from me ever again after our phone conversation five years earlier.

I had dreamed up two different ways to start the conversation. "I received a call from your daughter, Heather, the other day" or "Would you like to spy on your two adopted children?"

CHAPTER THIRTY-FOUR

THE MCMEETING

Saturday, September 17, 2005

I had an idea brewing about Darryl and Donna's meeting. And they wouldn't know a thing.

I decided to call Nancy. She had not denied the birth of Darryl to me, and I felt certain that if Donna's story was true she wouldn't deny being her mom either. Darryl, Donna, and I were set to meet up the next day in Strathroy. It would be so awesome if Nancy could just walk into McDonald's and anonymously watch her two adopted grown children meet each other. I was sure she would have changed so much over the years that even I wouldn't be able to recognize her from the picture I had of her from Dad's wallet. Even if I did, I wouldn't say a thing. I would make her a promise not to tell.

It had been ages since I'd spoken with Nancy, but I

decided to still give her last known number a shot. As I dialled the number, I thought back to our conversation and how she seemed confused about who I was. Even when I had said my father was Leonard Hawkins it hadn't helped. As the phone continued to ring, it suddenly hit me like a ton of bricks. She must have thought I was her long-lost adopted daughter Heather (now named Donna) calling for a reunion. It all made sense now and explained the bizarre phone conversation we had years ago.

A lady answered the phone after several rings, but it wasn't Nancy. I automatically switched gears and told her that I was a friend of Nancy's and we hadn't spoken in some time. She went on to tell me how she was Nancy's daughter-in-law, and Nancy and her husband had moved to Huntsville a few years back. I didn't even get a chance to ask for her new number before she gave it to me. I guess I must have sounded very believable.

So now I knew Nancy and her husband had moved a few years ago. This worried me a bit, as I immediately thought she may have been trying to run from her past. Maybe my last call to her had played on her mind. I wondered if she thought Darryl would contact her and try to become a part of her life. Little did she know she had nothing to worry about. With the move, though, my scheme was foiled. I had so wished Nancy could have been there for Donna and Darryl's first meeting, even if only to look on from afar and see how her children had grown into adults. I guess it wasn't meant to be.

The thought crossed my mind how Nancy may have hung up on me if I had tried to call her and discuss her past again. This wouldn't have helped Donna at all and may have pushed Nancy further away from revealing the truth about her unwanted pregnancies. So, at this point, I just decided to pass this new phone number on to Donna. If Nancy was her mother, this was between the two of them.

Sunday, September 18, 2005

The big day seemed to take forever to come, but once it did I was so excited. As I bustled around the house making sure I had Donna and Darryl's phone numbers tucked into my purse, I thought about how all this had transpired. If I hadn't gone looking for Darryl, Donna would never have found us. During our phone conversation, Donna had told me that she wouldn't date anyone born in 1967 just in case it was her half-brother. Now she wouldn't have to be concerned about that anymore.

Jim stayed home with Jason and was prepped to take him to hockey later that day. Darian came with me. As he got older, his interest in forming a relationship with his Uncle Darryl grew. His curiosity had been ignited when given the opportunity to meet Darryl's half-sister Donna. I was proud of him for supporting me through my search for Darryl, and for wanting to be there when they met. He was probably just as excited as me to see their faces when they finally connected.

I honestly could not begin to imagine how they felt growing up knowing they were given away for someone else to raise. As a mother, I was thankful to never be put in that position. To me, it seemed like an impossible choice. My wish for them that day was to find the peace and closure I did when I found Darryl. From there, it was up to them if they wanted to form a relationship.

Donna frantically waved Darian and I over to the table as soon as we walked into the McDonald's. She knew it was us from my description of myself and the fact I would be bringing my teenage son Darian. I immediately noticed Donna's crystal blue eyes and how they twinkled when she laughed. Her happiness was evident by her brilliant smile, which lit up her face for most of our visit. Her hair was dark and she would be considered of average height. I introduced Darian and we chatted a bit before Darryl strolled in. I motioned him over to our table and watched the expressions on both of their faces.

Darryl was smiling and seemed more comfortable with making eye contact for longer periods. I found that the more I got to know him the more at ease he seemed in conversation. Donna was in awe as she stared at Darryl. She was probably analyzing and comparing their physical characteristics, just as I did when I first met Darryl. I made the introductions, and then we decided to order our lunch.

When we returned to our table and began our meals, I facilitated the conversation at first, but then Darryl and

Donna took it from there. Their phone chats had them fairly caught up with their personal lives, so they quickly moved to talking about their physical appearances, as I had guessed.

Before I gave Darryl the pictures of his mom, our dad, and him as a baby, I had photocopied them. They had been the ones found in my father's wallet when he died. I gave Donna a copy of them for her to keep. She was thrilled she now had a picture of her mom to look at.

We talked about how Aunt Myrna had helped me immensely and Donna commented that it would be nice to meet her someday.

My aunt lived near this particular McDonald's, so I thought "Why not?" I love things that happen in the spur of the moment. "What better time than this?" I said to myself. I excused myself and told them I would be right back. I ran over to her house and luckily she was home.

"Oh, Wendy. What a surprise!" she exclaimed as she opened her door. We hugged as she led me inside.

"Hi, Aunt Myrna. Sorry. I apologize but I didn't have time to call first," I said.

"Oh, that's okay. I'm just so glad to see you. So what brings you over?" she asked.

"Well. You aren't going to believe this, but I have Darryl and Donna over at McDonald's right now, and Donna would love to meet you. I was wondering if you could spare a few minutes? Or are you busy?" I asked.

"No. Not right at the moment. Wow. This is all so

sudden. But of course, I'd love to come and see them."
I could tell how much she was taken by surprise, but
I was very thankful she agreed to play along at such
short notice.

She hurriedly got ready and then we headed over to
McDonald's. Once inside, introductions were made and
she sat down with us for the next hour. Her sometimes
red face and shaky voice revealed some of the emotional
impact Donna's questions had on her. She commented
on the uncanny resemblance between Donna and Nancy,
which of course made Donna beam.

This statement may have brought back some painful
memories for Aunt Myrna about her brother, my dad,
who was killed one fateful night. Nancy had been at the
Roby's the night of the shooting , and Myrna had witnessed all of their testimony at the inquiry. She had been
a young mom herself at that time, and she had wanted to
adopt her brother's baby boy even though circumstances
at the time made it impossible. Now when she looked at
Darryl, she was probably thinking he could have been
raised as her son.

The mystery of Donna's biological father was also
discussed that day, and I asked Aunt Myrna if she could
lend any thoughts. She had heard rumours of there being
another baby given up for adoption by Nancy, and she
told us the name of one possible man Nancy had been
seeing at the time.

I thanked Aunt Myrna for all her help and she headed

back home. For sure her day had been shaken up a bit, but I was so grateful for her help. I had felt she should be there for Donna and Darryl's meeting, as she had been such a crucial part of their story right from the beginning.

It was decided that since we were in the city where our dad and my stillborn baby were buried, a visit to the cemetery would be in order. Since I remembered the gravesite location, I led the way. After my Grandpa Hawkins had passed away in 1996, I remembered there was no longer just a footstone to mark the site of my dad and baby's grave. There was now an actual tombstone. The Hawkins family had added my dad's name to their headstone. "THEIR SON, LEONARD WESLEY, 1942-1967" had been inscribed below my grandparents' names. Grandpa's dates were both filled in after his death. Grandma's dates were not completed yet as she was still living.

I used to go searching for the site, and with only a little footstone marker to locate Alaric's gravesite it wasn't easy to find. That's where I knew my dad had been laid to rest and Alaric had been buried on top of him. With the tombstone in place, I appreciated being able to easily find them now. It also recognized my father's existence and, I bet, it helped him rest a little more peacefully. Nancy told me she used to go visit his gravesite and I often wondered how she found it before Alaric's marker was there. I shared this piece of information with both Darryl and Donna to help them know their mom as a woman who had loved this man enough to visit his grave and to help them remember where he was buried.

That visit had also been a day for Darian and me to remember Alaric, Darian's brother and my son. I honestly couldn't recall ever having taken Darian there before. Darian, never knowing Alaric, showed concern for what I must be feeling. It was impossible to grieve for something he never had or felt, but he knew of the pain I had been through. I had felt Alaric's kicks and turns and his growing body inside of mine. Then the blood. Then the loss. Alaric was, and always will be, a part of me "too good for this world," as my sister-in-law Barb had so beautifully expressed.

Darryl and Donna surely felt some closure that day, as we all parted ways. I told Donna about how I had called Nancy and discovered she had moved two years previously. I promised to send her the new phone number when I returned home. She had not yet tried to contact Nancy at this point, but was willing to do so when she had the chance. Darryl knew a bit more about his mother at this point since more details had been divulged. He still hadn't come right out and asked me her name, but I'm sure he picked up small, subtle hints during the conversations that day. Either way, he was likely about to find out. Donna could end up telling him and that was fine with me.

Darryl had a lot to think about as he drove home. He had met another half-sister and had seen his father's grave. Maybe he had thought that someday he would meet his mother and that would be the final act for providing closure. Could Donna be the catalyst needed to orchestrate such a grand finale?

CHAPTER THIRTY-FIVE

SIX DEGREES OF SEPARATION

Monday, September 19, 2005

9:58 PM Sent Email

From: Wendy Scott

To: Donna

Dear Donna,

My head's still spinning from yesterday! How about yours? Thank you so much for buying lunch. I think I forgot to say that yesterday with everything that was going on.

So what did you think of Darryl? Since I first met him, I feel he has changed a lot for the better. He seems more content and at ease with us. By the time we all said our good-byes, he looked quite happy, I thought.

Here's Nancy's new phone number: XXX-XXX-XXXX. I'd

appreciate it if you let me know what comes of it if you try to call her. Presently, I don't have any reason to call her so I'll just leave it at that.

Well, I better go as tomorrow comes all too soon.

Bye!

Love Wendy

Tuesday, September 20, 2005

8:32 AM Received Email

From: Donna

To: Wendy Scott

Wendy,

Well, my husband says to me, "You're beaming." I'll just say that Sunday was a fantastic day! After 37 years, it was well worth the wait. I can't believe how we chatted away the day! Thanks so much for setting it up and you're welcome for lunch—it's the least I could do for hogging your whole day! Special thanks to Darian for sharing his time, too. He's turning into quite the young man ... we had a great chance to chat while we were waiting for you and Aunt Myrna to join us.

She's quite the woman too. I hope our visit didn't upset her too much. I have sooooo many questions for her, but didn't want to overwhelm her. I also didn't want to talk about Mom when Darryl was there. If he's not ready to go there I understand.

Thanks for taking us to the cemetery. I hope that Darryl

got some peace to know where Dad and some of the family are.

Yes, it was a very informative day. And to find out that I look like my mom was a little bit unnerving to say the least. But to actually have a picture of her ... I think I've worn out my copy already!

I can't thank you enough. I actually called Alice MacDonald when I got home on Sunday night and we talked for half an hour. She thought it was great that we finally got together and I called her to thank her for all her hard work, too. If it wasn't for her website (Barrie Parent Finders), I'd still be looking for all of you.

To be honest, I'm still a little bit stunned, excited, nervous, elated, and a whack of other mixed emotions. Seeing Darryl smile was great! He's a funny guy. I'm glad he let us in. Boy, is he ever tall. I can't get over how much he looks like his father. It's nice that he's getting to know your kids, too. I tried calling you a couple of times, but I couldn't get through—the line was busy.

Well, I've got to go. Doctor's appointment this morning, yeah! Have to go to London for a couple of hours. Do the appointment, run some errands, etc.

Talk to you soon, sweetie.

Donna

Wednesday, September 21, 2005

The phone rang the following day, and I knew immediately

it was Donna. Having that new phone number meant she was just a phone call away from speaking with her mom.

Sure enough, she had placed the call. After speaking with Nancy, it was confirmed Donna was the child born as Heather Rose Gunness in London on October 21, 1968. Nancy admitted that she had become pregnant again, and as an unmarried teen had given the baby up for adoption. She pretty much said the same thing to Donna that she had to me. She would share any information Donna wanted to know and she thought about her adopted babies every day, but she didn't want to meet them.

She was breathless after telling me about their conversation and I was so happy to hear that Nancy was her mother. Donna was disappointed that Nancy was adamant about not wanting to meet her, but she was grateful for the information she shared. Nancy had returned to school at some point and had gotten an education. She had been retired from working for many years as a Process Engineer. Most certainly, furthering her education had been a step in the right direction and I was happy to hear of her hard work towards a well-earned retirement. Nancy's husband was also retired by this time.

2007

Donna and I maintained contact and would sporadically touch base with each other since meeting two years earlier. One time when Jason had a soccer game in Donna's home town, she met us at the field to cheer him on and we were able to do some catching up. She and Darryl had still been communicating and we would swap info about him to keep each other updated.

One late night call between Donna and me revealed an interesting connection. I truly believe there are a certain number of people separating us from one another. It's called "Six degrees of separation" and it has been proven to me over and over again. This time was no exception.

During a conversation about my father, Donna asked me how he had died. I carefully described the situation that led to his death and the family's house where it had taken place.

"My father was accidentally killed when he broke into the house where your mother was staying. He probably wanted to confront her about giving up baby Dwayne," I stated.

"Oh. You never told me this before. So where was my mother staying?" she asked.

"She was staying with one of my father's best friends. My mother and aunt both confirmed how odd it was that David Roby and his wife took Nancy into their home," I said.

"What did you say the name was again?" she questioned.

"David Roby," I replied.

"David Roby from London?" she asked.

"Yes. That's the one. The shooting took place in London," I confirmed.

Silence.

"Donna? Are you still there?" I thought we had lost our connection as normally our chatter is non-stop.

"Yes. Sorry. I'm just in shock. I know him," she replied.

"Are you sure it's the same David Roby? That would just be too weird." I stated.

"It has to be. He'd be around your dad's age. I met him through foster parenting."

Donna had previously told me about her role as a foster parent, and all the hard work and training involved in the process. Apparently, David and his wife had fostered children too and belonged to the same agency as Donna.

Now if you know Donna at all, you know she is very excitable and maybe a bit too forthcoming. She could also be described as being very knowledgeable and capable of handling herself in all situations. She likes helping the underdog and puts her own comfort on hold to address the needs of others. Having a military background, she is very direct and doesn't waste any time doing something once she sets her mind to it.

This time, she set her sights on calling David Roby and asking him about the night my dad was killed. She wanted to know everything he could tell her about her mother and about what happened that night. I knew it would be an interesting conversation and hoped it ended well for her. After all, she would be bringing up an experience for him that not only ended his best friend's life but also revealed a side of him she hadn't known about. It was information that he potentially wished she knew nothing about. I thought it just might change her overall opinion of him.

I waited with anticipation to see where this next clue would lead.

After my father was killed, life was like a roller coaster ride of emotions—full of ups and downs and twists and turns ... and I never knew what to expect around the corner. My thoughts as a very young child were centered around acceptance. I don't remember anyone asking me how I felt about my dad's death or if I missed him. "It's just the way it is" and "I shouldn't discuss my thoughts or feelings because it won't change a thing" were my ways of rationally putting thoughts of my dad aside. Then when I was a bit older, and looked around at other families with dads, I started to realize what I was missing. I questioned God about why he took my dad away from me.

As a teen, I had wanted to march right up to David Roby and confront him with what he had done. Didn't he realize I needed my dad to help me through tough times? Having no male figure in the household, I never witnessed an ongoing relationship between a man and a woman. When I started dating, I didn't know how to act, talk, or be myself around men, so I would just play shy. This made me feel insecure and I struggled with low self-esteem, eventually leading to attempted suicides. At that time in my life, I needed some useful coping mechanisms to help deal with the stresses of adolescence. I would read the newspaper article covering my father's death over and over again and become angrier each time.

There was no father to walk me down the aisle or to give his approval when I got married. I was on my own when determining a proper partner. No one ever told me to look for the essential qualities necessary for a successful relationship: respect, open-mindedness, collaboration, and empowerment. Mom's way of preparing us girls was to suggest we marry a Christian or a pastor of a church ... not that there's anything wrong with doing that. But obviously, there is much more to having a successful marriage than that.

After my first child, Darian, was born it hit home that my father would never see his children or grandchildren grow up. He had missed it all. So with a child of my own to teach about forgiveness, empathy for David started to worm its way into my thoughts. I began to open up to the idea that he had been a man protecting his family from a friend he knew to be a fighter who always won.

Years earlier when I had requested a copy of the inquest into my father's death I realized how a jury could have found David not guilty. My dad's death had been deemed an accident. I prayed for guidance from God. I wanted to forgive this man for what had happened. Only when I could find it in my heart to forgive would I truly be set free of this anger, hurt, and the feeling of being deprived of a father.

"I called him Wendy. I called and spoke with David Roby," Donna excitedly said.

"How did it go?" I asked.

"Well, I told him how I knew you and that I had found out about the death of your father. I then told him that Nancy is my mother. He was shocked to hear that," she said.

"Yes, no doubt. I would be too," I replied.

"We chatted about my mom because I wanted to know everything he could tell me about her and Leonard. Then I asked him about the baby."

I couldn't believe this. Wow! She had been brave.

"So what did he say about the baby?" I questioned.

"Wendy. He told me the baby was there the night of the shooting. Darryl was there that night!" she exclaimed.

"Really?" I asked.

"Yes. That's what he remembered. Nancy was there and so was the baby."

"The non-identifying information said he had been given up by Nancy and was placed in a temporary foster care home. Are you saying that was their home?" I asked.

"I'm just relaying what he remembers," she replied.

"The newspapers didn't mention a baby being in the house, only the three children," I stated.

"David and his wife have three children. I'm sure of that," she said.

"This is confusing, but something to possibly research in the future. For now, I'll just leave it alone. So how did your conversation with David end?" I asked.

"I don't think he likes me knowing so much about his personal life, especially the shooting. It does kind of change things between us. Oh well. It was well worth the call since now I know a little bit more about my mom and her history."

For years to come, I contemplated calling David myself to have a conversation about what went down on the early morning of July 22, 1967. I even discussed this with Donna and felt at first she was willing to share his information. Then, she must have thought better of it, so I didn't press her on the matter. I am sure after all the work I had put into tracking Darryl down, I could have easily found David's number. But something always stopped me.

During the writing of this book, I discovered that David had passed on. I wish I had reached out to him. I'll always wonder about his version of events surrounding my dad's death. My first question would have been why Nancy was there that night. And I'd want to know if baby Dwayne was with her. I wonder how the tragedy affected David and his family and how he tamed any runaway feelings of guilt ... if he had any. Somehow, he seemed able to come to terms with his actions and move forward with his life. Donna's claim that he and his wife fostered children suggests he was likely a kind and caring person. Regardless, I've forgiven him so I can move forward with my life as well.

Four uneventful years passed. Darryl, Donna, and I settled back into our normal lives and enjoyed routine calls and visits. The thrill of our big adventure eventually subsided. And then one day another unexpected phone call changed things. Again.

CHAPTER THIRTY-SIX

UNDERCOVER MEETING

July 2011

During the summer of 2011, I was enjoying my usual two months of vacation as a school board employee and celebrating my boys as they reached major milestones. Darian was off to post-secondary education in September, and Jason was well into high school. The previous year, due to some restructuring within the school board and union, I had lost my job. I decided to participate in the provincially funded program Second Careers, attended Lambton College, and obtained my Personal Support Worker certificate. Shortly after completing the course, I accepted a new position at Wallaceburg District Secondary School. Ironically, I ended up in the same role I had left the previous year.

After four years of intermittent contact with Donna, I

received a very unusual phone call from her that summer. Something was up; I could hear it in her voice and she rarely called in the middle of the week.

"So I just happened to be looking through the newspaper and guess what I came across?" Donna asked.

"No clue. What?" I replied.

"You aren't going to believe this. I came across a notice of Nancy's husband's memorial service. He died earlier this year and the memorial service is coming up this weekend. I'm thinking of going" she stated.

"Oh. Whereabouts is the service?" I asked.

"It's up north in Kearney. Remember that's where they moved to after retiring," she said.

"Yes. That's right. You did tell me that. So are you going to go?"

This would take a lot of courage and I wasn't sure how she was going to pull it off without being noticed.

"That's why I'm calling you. To run it by you and see what you thought," she said seriously.

"I think you should go and I wish I could go with you. What day is it?" I asked.

"It's this Saturday, July 23," she said.

"Oh darn, that's my birthday. I already have plans with Jim and the boys. Do you know someone else who can go?"

"Yes. My boyfriend said he'd go with me. He knows how important this is to me. I'm just so excited, Wendy. I'll get to see my mom and possibly my half-brothers," she exclaimed.

"So how will you go and not be noticed? And what will you say if someone asks you who the heck you are?" I sure hoped she knew what she was doing, otherwise this scheme could backfire. Nancy had made it really clear that she didn't want any contact.

"I'm just going to say I knew the deceased from somewhere. I'll make something up," she said mischievously.

"Oh, that's good, Donna. I'm so excited for you but a little scared too. Hopefully, Nancy doesn't recognize you. Remember how Aunt Myrna said you look a lot like her? Maybe wear sunglasses or something to hide those bright blue eyes of yours?" I laughed.

"Great idea! I'm also planning on leaving a letter with the Father officiating the service. I'll ask him to deliver it to Nancy a few days afterwards. Hopefully it will convince her how much I want to get to know her. Who knows? Maybe now that her husband has passed she'll change her mind about meeting me. It's worth a try," she said.

"You've thought of everything. I wish you the best of luck, Donna. I'll be waiting to hear how it all turns out."

The odds of Donna actually pulling this clandestine meeting off were not very high when I considered her impulsiveness. I wondered if she would be able to keep her identity a secret long enough to hand that letter to the priest. I sure hoped Nancy didn't recognize her, or that could end all hopes of her ever having any kind of relationship with her birth mother. Donna was risking it all to catch a glimpse of her mom and half-brothers. I wondered if this covert operation would be worth it.

July 25, 2011

The suspense was killing me. I finally broke down and called Donna to see if she had pulled off her plan without revealing her identity.

"Hi, Donna. So did you go?" I asked.

"Yes, I did, and it was so worth it, Wendy. I got to see my mom, half-brothers, and their wives and children. It was sooooooo great!" she shared enthusiastically.

"So what was your mom like?" I questioned.

"I can't believe how much I look like her. We have the same eyes. She didn't suspect a thing. Of course, we didn't get a chance to talk, and I probably would have blown my cover anyways," she responded.

"Did anybody ask why you were there?" I asked.

"Yes, and I just said I was a co-worker of the deceased. Nobody suspected a thing," she answered. "I also left my letter with the Father, asking him to deliver it to Nancy in a week or so. That way, it gives her some time to reflect after the memorial service. He was more than happy to do this when I explained to him who I was," she said.

"I sure hope that letter has an impact on her, Donna. What did the letter say?" I asked.

"Mostly it was updating her on things since we had last spoken on the phone. I told her that I had left the letter while at the memorial service and how I had actually seen her in person. I emphasized how important it was for her and I to meet someday. I can only hope she wants the same now that her husband has passed. He could have been the reason why she didn't want contact," she said positively.

"I was always under the impression Nancy didn't want her sons to know about her past so that was why she kept her distance. I could be wrong, though," I stated.

"Yes. Her boys could be the deciding factor now. If they don't know about her past and they find out about me and Darryl that could change things between them. Let's just cross our fingers and hope for the best," she said.

I doubted Donna would ever hear back from Nancy, and if she did, it would be to tell her to back off. Her past was something she wanted to run from, not run towards. Of course, I was basing this on how she had made it abundantly clear she didn't want to meet Darryl if I found him. I had hoped she would change her mind once I had connected with Darryl and shared with her what a good man he had become. Sadly, that hadn't been the case. Would things turn out differently for Donna?

November 2011

By fall 2011, the boys and I had all gone back to school in some capacity. Jason attended high school in Petrolia, I remained at the same school in an L.T.O. (Long Term Occasional) position, and Darian decided the engineering program at Western University wasn't for him and headed to Lambton College for the CPET (Chemical Production and Power Engineering Technology) course. The company Jim worked for folded, so he went from being a high-pressure water operator to being an AZ/DZ transport truck driver. This meant he could be gone for days at a time if he was tasked with long-haul runs; it all depended on the company he was working for at the time. Our family had some adjusting to do as we weren't used to Jim being gone for long periods of time.

It had been four months since Donna had attended the memorial in Kearney and left the letter for Nancy. With all the changes that had been going on for me, Jim, and the boys I had almost forgotten about Donna's latest adventure. So at first I was just pleasantly surprised to hear from her and had thought it would just be a casual call. I had thought wrong. She had good news. No. Make that fantastic news.

Nancy had called her.

CHAPTER THIRTY-SEVEN

SURPRISE REUNIONS

November 2011

Donna's visit to the memorial service and her letter had impacted Nancy enough for her to make contact. They had talked on the phone and Donna mentioned that Nancy had been quite honest, open, and communicative. She seemed to want to share more information and admitted that she had been afraid to get close to Donna while her husband was still alive. Now that he had passed, she felt less restricted and could speak openly about her past.

Nancy revealed the name of Donna's biological father, Terry, and explained that he had been born in Bermuda. This would be a substantial piece of information for Donna to start another search.

Their phone conversation lasted for quite some time, so long that even the Robys eventually came up. Donna told Nancy about her involvement with them as foster parents through the London C.A.S. She also shared the conversation she had with David Roby about Nancy, baby Dwayne, and the night of the shooting.

So now everything was out in the open. Nancy had nothing to hide and both of her adopted children had met me and each other. "Would the three of them ever meet?" I wondered.

For Donna, meeting both her birth parents in person would be the ultimate experience. For this to happen, though, her birth father would have to still be alive, unlike mine and Darryl's. For Darryl, the dream of meeting both parents would never come true. But he could reunite with Nancy if she ever agreed to meet him.

Immediately after hanging up with Nancy, Donna searched for her biological father on social media. At first she had no luck, but Donna switched up her approach as she knew most people used nicknames, versions of their first and second names, or different spellings of their surname on social media. She tried various combinations of his name until finally she hit the jackpot on Facebook. She had found a Terry in Bermuda who sure seemed to fit the bill. Within an hour Donna had found her dad. The internet sure can be a powerful tool when searching for a loved one.

After vetting and contacting Terry, they agreed to meet in person. They struck a fast friendship, but before long Donna realized her biological father was homeless and living out of his car. Due to her kind and generous nature, Donna took Terry into her home and he lived with her and her family for six months.

During that time, Donna and Terry had plenty of opportunities to discuss Nancy and how great it would be for them to have a reunion after all these years. Donna shared Nancy's phone number with Terry and he proceeded to contact her. He never let on that he knew Donna or where he had gotten Nancy's number from. As far as Nancy knew, Terry had somehow tracked her down on his own.

During Terry and Nancy's conversations, Donna of course came up. She was the thread that tied them together. Terry was a huge proponent of Nancy meeting Donna but Nancy was still a little hesitant. Maybe one day, though, she would be ready to reunite with Terry. They hadn't seen each other in approximately forty-five years, but they had once loved each other. Perhaps their curiosity would get the better of them.

Donna was over the moon when Nancy called and shared that she was ready to meet her and suggested they get together in Kearney. But Donna was also ecstatic because she had another plan up her sleeve. Her mom would be so surprised!

The big surprise was Terry! Nancy had no idea that when she opened her door that day to reunite with her daughter that it wouldn't be just the two of them reconnecting. She must have been speechless when she saw Terry was there as well. Boy, would I have loved to be a fly on the wall at that reunion. My wings would have been vibrating and tingling with all the emotional electricity in the room.

After explanations and hugs all around, Donna settled in to observe her surroundings and her parents. Her mom had retired to a beautiful cabin in the woods, a serene spot surrounded by nature. Nancy was a good sport about the situation and happy to finally meet Donna and possibly rekindle her relationship with Terry after all these years. Donna could hardly believe she was in the same room with both of her biological parents. This day had been a long time coming and she was going to enjoy every minute of it. She took in all the similarities, all the family history, and shared her life with them. It would be a day forever etched in her mind.

When I asked Donna what it was like meeting her mom for the first time she said, "Holy cow! Holy crap! Oh my god! It was like having a twin. We like the same colours, have the same eyeglass frames, and dress similarly. She even had saltwater taffy in her living room and I love it. We both like hickory sticks. It was surreal!"

Things went so well between Nancy and Terry that they decided to give it a serious go. They lived together for three years before Nancy decided to end the relationship. It must not have lived up to her expectations. It had been many years since their first relationship, if you could even call it that, and maybe it just was never meant to be.

Before Terry's departure, though, another wonderful reunion transpired. Someone else visited that beautiful cabin in Kearney for the first time. Someone maybe not willing to admit they had been waiting for this moment all their life. Someone who tried their best to appear uninterested. Yes. Darryl finally went to meet his mother.

Once Terry had settled in with Nancy, Donna decided to push things with Nancy a little bit further. She discussed with Darryl how things had progressed with their mom and felt Nancy was ready to take the final step. Together, they arranged a "surprise visit" and hoped everything would work out.

Donna and her boyfriend arrived at Nancy's place first, as planned. Donna was going to introduce the "what if" scenario of bringing Darryl with her sometime to meet their mother and see how she responded. Nancy and Donna had talked about Darryl previously, but she had still never wanted to meet him. But Donna realized Nancy wasn't home from town yet, so only Terry was there to greet them. "Darn. Maybe things won't go as planned after all," Donna thought. Darryl arrived next, beating Nancy to the cabin. Not to spoil the surprise, Donna made him wait on the back steps, out of sight, until Nancy arrived home. I am not sure how they hid his car. I guess they could have said it was Donna's boy-friend's car.

When she arrived, Terry helped Nancy with the grocery bags and then she came in to greet her guests. Donna must have been ready to burst with excitement and worry. It would have been difficult for her to contain herself and hold it together long enough to put her plan into action. When Donna asked her the big question, Nancy said she would like to meet Darryl sometime, which was a good thing seeing as he was hiding on the back stairs waiting to meet her! After hearing this, Donna made something up about needing an item from the car and went outside. Ta-da! She came back in with Darryl.

Donna shared that Nancy was astounded and over-joyed by her surprise. She had not seen her baby boy since giving him up for adoption in 1967. I wondered what it was like for her at the London C.A.S. that day. Did she look back to catch one last glimpse of her blonde-haired, blue-eyed baby boy? To walk out the door knowing you'd never see your child again … I don't know how she did it. She's a stronger person than I am. I think that would be the most heart-wrenching, horrific experience for any parent to endure.

Before Nancy's eyes, Darryl transformed from baby to toddler, to child, to adolescent, to adult, to parent. Never had she witnessed his tears after falling and scraping a knee, comforted him after one of his worst nightmares, enjoyed his laughter after sharing a joke, or cuddled with him while reading his favourite bedtime stories. Nancy had missed so much of Darryl's life … she must have wondered how they could ever bridge the gulf between them. But she did have one special claim. She was his birth mom.

To finally see and meet her first-born son must have felt like an enormous weight being lifted off Nancy's shoulders. All the regrets and worries were gone. Darryl was there and nothing else mattered. She rushed to him and embraced him with a lifetime of hugs.

This final reunion meant my part of their journey had come to an end. There would be no more stepping stones for me to find. The four had finally come together and would now have the opportunity to forge their own path.

PART FOUR
CLOSING

CHAPTER THIRTY-EIGHT

THE SUN SETS ON THE GOLDEN GIRLS

2014

B ut sadly while one family grows its roots, another loses its last member. I haven't mentioned them in a while, but over the years The Golden Girls of my life had gone from three down to one. My second moms were slowly leaving me for their eternal home with Jesus Christ our Lord and Saviour. Dorothy, A.K.A. Red, was the last survivor. Miss Barber (age 82) had passed away in 2004 and Jean (age 87) in 2011. My eulogy at Jean's funeral brought tears and laughter to the many grieving friends and family in attendance. The words came easily, as Jean meant the world to me. I wanted to express my thoughts and feelings in public in hopes it would help me get closure. It was a great send-off for a remarkable woman.

The parsonage had been my refuge while growing up. In a house where being the stubborn, middle child often meant feeling left out, I had to feel important somewhere. That somewhere was with my Golden Girls. A call would be placed and they always understood my need for escape. After I had my fill of their undivided attention for the weekend, I would return home feeling renewed and energized ... and maybe even a little bit spoiled.

Dorothy, after losing her two best friends, became a different person. For starters, she had to live alone for the first time in her life. I was seeing a more vulnerable side to her. Tears, fears, and wanting advice from me wasn't like the Dorothy I had known for most of my life. But then the other two ladies had always been front and centre for me, while she had remained quietly in the background. But after their passing, she became my main focus.

Dorothy had never attained a driver's license so she was always at the mercy of others. Whenever someone asked her to go somewhere with them, she always jumped at the chance. She told me that she didn't want to miss out on any opportunities that came her way. As a result she had emerged from her cocoon, spreading her wings and flying wherever the wind carried her.

We continued to visit back and forth and Dorothy would even stay with me and my family at our home on St. Clair Parkway. One year while in her eighties, she was determined to help Jim shingle the carport roof at the back of our garage and weed the garden. "I can just climb the ladder and hand him the shingles," she said. I thanked her, but said Jason could help his dad with that. We visited the garden instead, where she did pull a few weeds and pick some vegetables for supper … and was thankfully much closer to the ground than she had first intended.

Our friendship grew deeper with each passing year and I truly appreciated the time I spent with her. It was like a gift from God for us to have these years together and to be able to support one another. She remained a true friend who listened non-judgmentally and encouraged me in all my endeavours.

Dorothy passed away in 2017 (age 88) shortly after she had started living like a queen in a retirement home. I had teased her that it was comparable to staying in a luxury hotel after I surveyed the elegant decor, sampled the quality cuisine, and learned about the wonderful weekly housekeeping service.

With Dorothy's death the sun set on the Golden Girls. But just like at Jean's funeral I was honored to deliver the eulogy. Speaking at Dorothy's funeral I managed to not only fully celebrate all she had offered to the world, but also I included the other two ladies as well, saying goodbye to them all, somewhat assuaging my grief with the knowledge that life on earth is fleeting but they would be together for eternity in Heaven.

Before they knew it, Darryl and Donna would also be grappling with the fleeting nature of life and great loss.

The Golden Girls visiting us in Inwood.
Left to right - Dorothy, Miss Barber, and Jean.

CHAPTER THIRTY-NINE

WAS IT WORTH IT?

2019

Both Donna and Darryl had the chance to enjoy a few good years with their birth mother. They had years of lost time to make up for, so they crammed in as much time together as possible to get to know each other. More than likely, many late nights were spent in conversations—conversations with an undercurrent of regret for not having found each other sooner.

After Terry left, Nancy became ill. Adam, one of her sons, went and lived with her to help out. One morning near the end of 2015, Nancy just never woke up. The cause of death was unknown, but a heart attack was suspected to be the culprit. All four of Nancy's children attended her memorial service and felt comfortable enough with each other that they all stood together for a photo.

After Terry and Nancy's relationship ended, he fell into his old habits. In particular, he struggled to keep his diabetes in check. Donna let me know that in early 2016 Terry had died from the effects of diabetes; it was only around five months after Nancy's death.

Donna has told me on a few occasions that when her parents died she felt like they had been torn away from her far too soon. She especially regretted losing her mom. Her relationship with Nancy had just started to grow into a real friendship and then she was gone. One night over the phone, she shared, "I feel so cheated. I finally had my mom in my life and she was taken away so fast. It still hurts like it was yesterday. Not many things have affected me like this, but losing her again has been devastating."

Most of us have lost a loved one and know that we work through the stages of grief—denial, anger, bargaining, depression, and acceptance—in our own time. Unfortunately for some, acceptance can never be attained if certain emotional needs aren't met. Maybe this was the case with Donna and Darryl. Had they had enough time with their mom to get some of the love and closure they needed? Darryl doesn't really talk much about Nancy's death, but he does admit that he misses her. He said that he became quite comfortable calling her "Mom" and enjoyed the little bit of time he got to spend with her. To him, building a relationship with his mom "was wonderful." I asked him once if it was worthwhile for us to meet and for him to forge the short-lived connection he had with his mom. He replied, "Yes. It's been awesome. I'm just not very good at talking about it or reaching out."

During all her grief, Donna has found refuge in an unexpected place. She promised Nancy she would "take care of her boys" if anything should happen to their mother. She has been sticking to her word and helping Adam and Jason in any way she can. Donna has formed a close relationship with Jason, Nancy's youngest son from her only marriage. Donna's mission has been to help Jason through some of life's unexpected challenges. Maybe in the process, she is learning more about their mother from Jason, making it a win-win situation.

Terry had stayed in touch with Jason and Adam up until the time of his passing. He may have developed a connection with them, or just felt the need to offer his support as they worked through their parents' deaths. During the few years she had with her birth father, Donna learned she had another half-brother named Joshua. He was Terry's son from another relationship. She also confided to me how she and Terry were not on the best of terms when he died because he hadn't seemed to fully support the relationship she was building with her mom. Maybe he wanted Nancy all to himself? Who knows.

Knowing all of these things has left me with a deep sadness for Donna. At the time of writing this, she has health issues and is experiencing real physical pain. Let's hope her back surgery happens sooner rather than later. It's difficult to watch someone go from being absolutely elated to utter despondency. I remember her being so ecstatic the day she met Darryl and me. She was literally vibrating with excitement. Maybe one day I will see that same happiness and glint in her eye, perhaps after she has entered that final stage: acceptance. Until then, I pray for her every day and ask God to give her the guidance and hope she needs to carry on through her physical and mental pain.

Now that my search is over and so many lives have been affected because of it, I have lots to reflect on. Was it a gift or a curse for Donna and Darryl to find their parents only to lose them again so soon? Did it give them closure? Or open up too many old wounds? Darryl was a missing piece of my father I felt led to find. Finding him provided me with the closure I longed for. Meeting Donna and the story that unfolded from that was a surprise bonus. She lists me as "sister" on Facebook, so I gained that honour for the third time in my life and I know that us meeting has been a positive thing in her life. Without me, she would never have met Darryl, her mom, or her dad. Plus it never hurts to have more sisters.

Donna, Darryl, and I all keep in touch. Quite a few years back, Darryl had some heart issues. Wanda and I visited him during one of his hospital stays and were amazed at his bravery. His playful nature suggested he enjoyed the attention of the pretty nurses. Donna, being her usual helpful self, found out about his hospital stay and before long was stopping by for visits and then later dropped Darryl off meals at home. After some lifestyle changes, such as eating healthier, I'm happy to report that Darryl is doing much better.

You know how people usually complain that social media can isolate people from the real world? Well, I've seen the opposite given how it's helped integrate Darryl into my life. I've noticed Donna, Wanda, Linda, Darian, and Jason commenting on Darryl's occasional posts. It's so nice to see that my family has welcomed him into their lives and accepted him. Aunt Myrna has even connected with him on Facebook. Darryl told me once, "Aunt Myrna is a very cool lady and always comments on any of my posts." The feeling is mutual as she has expressed to me over the years how much she's enjoyed getting to know Darryl. Along with staying in touch through Facebook, special events such as birthdays and Christmas warrant meeting up with Darryl in person. We even sometimes get together to catch up over a fabulous meal at one of our favourite restaurants at the time. He still labours as a tinsmith and is a grandfather two times over now, so I see a more mature side trying to emerge during his proud musings. I have yet to have the joy of becoming a grandmother, but I look forward to it whenever God feels the time is right.

Was my search for Darryl worth it? You bet it was. It changed all our lives forever and brought closure to a few secrets. Even more, it empowered me to believe that "I can do all things through Christ who strengthens me" (Philippians 4:13, New King James Version).

CHAPTER FORTY

FINDING MY VOICE

All of my life I have struggled to be self-empowered and to not let mental health issues get the best of me. What happened to my dad was indeed a tragedy. The choices he made deeply affected the lives of many people, including me. His death July 22, 1967 has played a role in my mental health. But I remind myself it is hereditary like many other diseases and I have chosen not to use it as an excuse for the way my life has turned out. Instead, I continually seek help from friends, family, and professionals to cope and become the best version of me I can be. With each new relationship I develop, I realize my growth and can learn something new about myself, whether it be good or bad. My bouts of anxiety and depression are short-lived now that I know how to "harness" it, much like Darryl says about his ADHD.

Finding Darryl was an inconceivable accomplishment.

Even though I knew it was a longshot, my stubborn nature would never allow me to give up. The good that came from this journey was well worth the risk. I felt the daily support of family, friends, and God. Romans 8:31 asks if God is for us, then who can ever be against us? He was and is on my side at all times.

Luckily, my story turned out for the best. But if it hadn't I knew where to turn for help. If you should find yourself in a situation where you feel compelled to find a loved one, please keep the following in mind:

1. Know where to access help should you need emotional support before or after meeting a lost loved one.

2. Think about what you want from the relationship and ease into it gently. The other party may not want the same as you or may have different motives for your new-found relationship.

3. Feel the person out. Use your gut instinct as to whether this is something you want to continue or not.

4. Investigate all possibilities and accept the facts. This person could be deceased, incarcerated, or have a history of violence and abuse.

5. If you are an adoptee, your biological parent could reject or abandon you, and in worse case scenarios they could even abuse you.

If after considering all of these possibilities you still want to go ahead with your search, then by all means do so. Like I've said before, finding Darryl has provided me with closure after losing my father and a stillborn baby.

This book has empowered me to do some critical self-exploration and to grow as a person. Through writing, I have "come into my own" and found my voice, and as a result I've conquered one of my greatest fears: public speaking. Being the author of the material I was delivering at church, weddings, parties, and funerals, I could spend countless hours choosing the exact words to express my sincere thoughts. God helped me realize that what I wanted to say was worthwhile and afforded me the talent to write the words and the self-esteem to deliver my message with ease and grace. And yes, the encouragement and compliments afterwards didn't hurt either.

Writing has given me the self-confidence I've been chasing all my life. Once I send my work out into the world, I know it's out of my hands. Make of it what you will: "Here I am, world. Take it or leave it. Either way, I'm me now and I like myself."

CHAPTER FORTY-ONE

NEGATIVES AND POSITIVES

Sunday, June 16, 2019

I can feel it creeping up inside of me but can't do any-thing about it. As I enter my place of worship today, I try to avoid eye contact. This way I don't have to answer that tedious question, "How are you today?" I always reply, "I'm okay," when really I'm not.

My head has been swirling with negative thoughts and emotions since I woke up. It's Father's Day, and most years it's still a struggle to get through the day. My mind tells me to be with people, but I keep fighting it by mak-ing excuses and thinking to myself, "You're too grouchy and depressed to be around people. They are going to notice, and you don't want to pass this awful feeling on."

I feel small in my pew. Even with people on either

side of me, loneliness is lodged deep within my soul. When I'm "fine" my head is held high, conversation comes easily, and I actually want to interact with others. Not today. One lady, upon leaving the church, notices my different demeanour and asks me if I'm alright. I question, "How did you know?"

She answers, "I could tell by the way you walked." Her advice was to pray, which I did all the way to the gym.

On the way, I swallow the big lump in the back of my throat. You know ... the one that comes just before tears. There. I stopped them.

My workout is good, and thankfully there is no forced small talk. I focus on my routine as old rock and roll pumps through my earbuds. Gradually the negative thoughts and emotions diminish.

As I walk back to my car, a feeling of peace and contentment washes over me. Magically, I transform into my old self!

For those of you who have never experienced mental health issues, just stop reading now. You don't understand what a big win it is to free yourself from the grips of anxiety or depression. For those of you who "get it," who have felt so small and have just wanted to melt into your seat, please remember these few simple things that can change your mood, your day, and your life:

1. Pray to the one who loves you.

2. Exercise any way you can, until you work up a sweat.

3. Reach out to people who care about you, no matter if your mind tells you how insignificant you are and no one cares. They do!

4. Do something you love.

5. Plan things and follow through, even if it's just one thing each day.

6. Take care of your health. Get lots of sleep and eat healthily.

Remember what you were taught in school about negatives and positives? How you need to add positives to negatives to make them positive again? Please don't let your negatives become so low that you can't add enough positives to balance things out. Use the six steps above until you're firmly in the positives. To end this little story, I have to tell you one more awesome thing that happened. Two wonderful friends of mine stopped by today to take me for a long walk. Of course, I accepted and mentioned how wonderful it was to see them as I'd been feeling a bit depressed. Their visit added more positives to my negatives.

So there you have it. Prayer, exercise, and good friends. All this gal needs to change her day. And don't forget to ask yourself. "How can I add some positives to those around me?" That's something I forgot to add to the list. Few things feel as wonderful as lifting up those around me by helping to get them back to the positive side of that number line.

January 2020

I sit at my counter-height kitchen table, tapping away at the keys on my computer and listening to Christian worship videos on YouTube. Out the window, snow blows across the light streaming from the street lights. Looks like the winter snow may stay for a while. It's the beginning of a new year but the final chapter of my story.

Things have changed a lot for me over the past six years. Even though I tried my best to save our relationship, Jim and I grew apart and eventually divorced. I wanted a change of scenery so I moved to a historic little oil town called Petrolia. Sometimes it has been tough being on my own, but like with Dorothy, the experience has helped me grow. Also, I have become stronger in my faith, leaning on the One who promises to be with me always—God.

The boys, now both out on their own, visit often. In addition to their day jobs, they have formed an EDM (Electronic Dance Music) group where they collaborate to produce some of the best original beats and remixes in the genre. I love seeing them when they are together as it's evident they are best friends. They bring out the best in one another.

May the words in this book reach you at a time when they are of some use. And here's hoping you are open to really hearing them. My goal has always been to help others by sharing what I have learned. Sometimes that learning has come from heartache, suffering, anxiety, and depression ... but whatever doesn't kill you makes you stronger. Right?

In this book, you have followed my journey as I grew from a shy four-year-old girl with no self-confidence into a bold, empowered woman who stopped at nothing to find her half-brother. I hope you found the journey was worth the ride, and that you learned no matter what life sends your way, with enough faith, strength, and determination you can prevail.

I am a living testament.

TIMELINE OF EVENTS

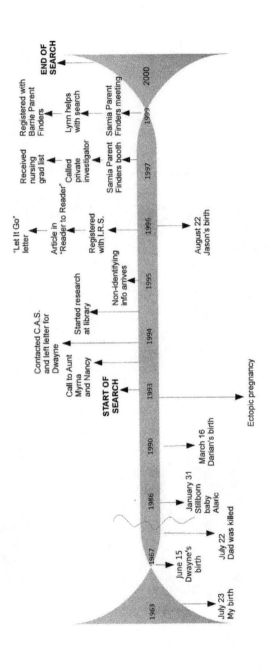

Timeline of Events

1963 — July 23 My birth

1967 — June 15 Dwayne's birth; July 22 Dad was killed

1986 — January 31 Stillborn baby Alaric

1990 — March 16 Darian's birth

1993 — START OF SEARCH; Call to Aunt Myrna and Nancy; Ectopic pregnancy

1994 — Contacted C.A.S. and left letter for Dwayne; Started research at library

1995 — Non-identifying info arrives

1996 — "Let It Go" letter; Article in "Reader to Reader"; Registered with I.R.S.; August 22 Jason's birth

1997 — Received nursing grad list; Called private investigator; Sarnia Parent Finders booth

1999 — Registered with Barrie Parent Finders; Lynn helps with search; Sarnia Parent Finders meeting

2000 — END OF SEARCH

ACKNOWLEDGMENTS

This book is based on a baby given up for adoption in 1967; my half-sibling. For many years, the search engulfed my life. Evidence of this is contained in a brown manilla envelope, stuffed full of information, names, dates, newspaper clippings, and scrap pieces of paper. If it wasn't for that child, there would be no story so I start by thanking that person for being born.

In the early stages of the search, I thank my ex-husband Jim for being so supportive and my boys Darian and Jason for being there when I needed a hug, kiss, or reason for getting up every day. You two boys are my everything.

My sisters, Wanda and Linda, have been my emotional support throughout my life so I thank them for always being there when I needed them. They encouraged me on my journey to write this book and fielded any doubts I may have had about my abilities in completing this huge undertaking.

Aunt Myrna and Mom were my go-to people for any information about Dad. They lived the story and helped me understand some of the history, conversations, and character traits I never knew about Dad. Thank you ladies.

Lynn Clark, you are someone I still have yet to meet. Your kindness and generosity towards me, a stranger, will never be forgotten. Thank you.

Donna, you were an unexpected but wonderful encounter that added another part to my book. I would like to express my gratitude for the many hours you spent answering my questions and being readily available for each chat.

Dr. Eva Shaw told me I was a writer, and now I believe her. The feedback on every assignment was both positive and encouraging. Please continue to teach your students the way you taught me ... with your heart.

Two authors, I had the pleasure of meeting, have been my mentors since the initial idea of this creation. They took time out of their own busy careers to guide me down the path and lead me into this lonely, but rewarding world of writing. Their expertise and knowledge led me step by step in every process so I am sincerely grateful to Daniel Barton and Gloria Pearson-Vasey for all their help.

My beta readers deserve a round of applause for all their hard work. Your critical feedback and support kept me writing during all of life's moments. May ample credit be given to my earliest readers, Wanda Pratt, John Lean, and Kendra McDonald who were there at the beginning stages. Kim Gleason and Wilma Luth you showed your dedication by enduring several drafts and encouraging me towards the editing process.

Last, but definitely not least, my editor Christine Penhale made this book into something great. Each week, you dove into the book and amazed me with your attention to detail, understanding my thoughts, and ways you made the story flow. Thank you for all your time, encouragement, and help.

ABOUT THE AUTHOR

Wendy L.Scott-Hawkins is a full-time Educational Assistant, mother of two adult children, an avid walker, and a Scrabble enthusiast. She uses her life experiences to craft her talent of writing from the heart. *Searching For a Stranger and Finding Myself - A Memoir* is her first novel.